SHUT UP AND LISTEN!

THE TRUTH ABOUT HOW TO COMMUNICATE AT WORK

THEO THEOBALD AND CARY COOPER

KOGAN PAGE

London and Sterling, VA

First published in Great Britain and the United States in 2004 by Kogan Page Limited
Reprinted 2004

120 Pentonville Road
London N1 9JN
UK
www.kogan-page.co.uk

22883 Quicksilver Drive
Sterling VA 20166–2012
USA

© Theo Theobald and Cary Cooper, 2004

ISBN 0 7494 4024 4

British Library Cataloguing-in-Publication Data

A CIP record for this book is available from the British Library.

Library of Congress Cataloging-in-Publication Data

Theobald, Theo, 1957–
 Shut up and listen! : the truth about how to communicate at work / Theo
Theobald and Cary Cooper.
  p. cm.
 Includes index.
 ISBN 0-7494-4024-4
1. Communication in management. 2. Communication in organizations. 3.
Business communication. I. Cooper, Cary L. II. Title.
 HD30.3.T453 2004
 650'.01'4–dc22   2003028085

Typeset by Saxon Graphics Ltd, Derby
Printed and bound in Great Britain by Clays Ltd, St Ives plc

Contents

About the authors   *iv*

Preface   *v*

Introduction   1

PART 1   Insight   5

1   **Revelations**   7
The truth about honesty, charisma, storytelling and more

2   **What kind of communicator are you?**   26
The truth about your individual style

PART 2   How to...   39

Introduction   41

3   **The truth about reading**   47
How to, when to. Getting the most out of what you read

4   **The truth about writing**   54
Context, grammar, tone of voice and use of Plain English

5   **Persuasion**   71
Learn through advertising – read the case study – try it for yourself

6   **Writing – the rules of the tools**   86
How to write e-mail, text and Web copy

7   **Listening**   103
How and when

8   **Talking**   111
How and when

9   **Listening and talking – the rules of the tools**   117

10   **Feeling**   141
First impressions, body language, culture

PART 3   Planning for success   159

11   **Planning**   161
Auditing, ditching the time wasters, targeting and achieving

12   **Six simple strategies**   178
Ways to implement your plan

Appendix I   Further recommended reading   *182*

Appendix II   A list of contributors   *183*

Index   *185*

About the authors

Theo Theobald has made a career out of communication – seeing the benefits of it being done well and witnessing the aftermath of it at its worst. A former BBC executive, radio copywriter and marketing manager, his has been more than a casual study from the sidelines. As a front line salesperson he quickly got to grips with the concept of tailoring the message to the audience: writing literally thousands of commercials for radio taught him how to get to the core of the message and make it lively and interesting, while a formal marketing background helped him to understand the need to plan what we say and how we say it.

More recently he has turned his attention to writing Web sites, producing business training materials and interviewing top business leaders and academics. This collaboration with Professor Cooper is a result of those endeavours.

You can find out more about Theo's writing, public speaking and communications training activities by visiting www.shutupand.co.uk.

Cary L Cooper CBE, is Professor of Organizational Psychology and Health at the Lancaster University Management School, Lancaster University, UK.

A distinguished academic and popular communicator, Cary has long been fascinated by what makes us tick and, more importantly, what doesn't. This has made him a leading authority on stress at work and beyond. The author of over 100 books on management and organizational psychology topics, he writes regularly for the national and specialist press and is a frequent guest on radio and television, where his views are sought on a range of business issues and on life in general.

He is a Fellow of the British Psychological Society, The Royal Society of Arts, The Royal Society of Medicine, The Royal Society of Health, an Academician of the Academy for the Social Sciences, the President of the British Academy of Management, a Companion of the Chartered Management Institute and one of the first UK-based Fellows of the American Academy of Management. He is also the President of the Institute of Welfare Officers, Vice President of the British Association of Counselling, an Ambassador of the Samaritans and Patron of the National Phobic Society.

Preface

If you're in a position where people are relying ever more heavily on your ability to articulate your ideas, marshal your resources and achieve your joint objectives then better communication is critical.

This book contains the collected wisdom and experience of over 20 individuals who have become experts in communication, from business, academic life and beyond. We asked their opinions, to make sure that any theories we put forward actually work in practice. We wanted to be sure that this is how real people really communicate in real situations.

As authors, our own experiences vary widely. Cary Cooper is a professor of Organizational Psychology and he's spent his academic career studying and researching the things that make us tick, like motivation, and the things that don't, like stress. Theo Theobald is an ex-advertising copywriter and former BBC executive who spent much of his career trying to solve the communications problems of his own organization and other people's.

During the course of researching and writing the book we made a number of surprising discoveries about some key aspects of communication. We uncovered an intriguing paradox too, despite the impact of technology, which has changed some communication channels out of all recognition; there remains an astounding simplicity within the core principles, which have stayed the same for generations.

With all of the practical issues we cover, we've tried to take a step back to find what's really going on. So just what is the significance of e-mail, what are the risks of text messaging, or even the expectations others might have of us when it comes to spelling, grammar and use of plain language?

Ultimately, we don't think that great communication is that difficult and yet despite that, an awful lot of people still seem to get it horribly wrong, so for your entertainment (and enlightenment) there are some examples of this later in the book.

More than anything we hope you enjoy the book and benefit from communicating more effectively.

Introduction

The truth about... how this book works

'It seems that if you have an organization with more than about seven people then lines of communication can become extended and messages can become confused.'

Michael Broadbent – Director of Group Corporate Affairs,
HSBC Holdings plc

We are much better communicators when we **know** more about ourselves, **think** about how and what we communicate and **act** according to the changes in our circumstance and environment. These are the principles this book is based on.

So, there are three main sections, starting with a short course in self-awareness so that you can find out more about the type of communicator (and person) you are, which is important if you're going to understand better how your various 'audiences' see you.

The main part of the book (the second section) is all about 'how to...'

Lots of business books talk a lot about strategy (the plan), but leave you feeling hungry for tactics (the day-to-day things you have to do to implement it). Here, we think you know your organization's plan better than we do, so all we're trying to do is give you advice on the best way to put it into practice.

There are five main subsections within 'how to...' looking at reading, writing, listening, talking and feeling, where you'll find tips on everything from how to persuade your boss to give you a company car, through to the best use of PowerPoint in a formal presentation.

We're grateful to the experts who contributed to this book; they all did so, giving their own time and experience freely. Lots of the practical stuff comes from them and we've added our own case studies and stories that we've collected over our own careers in business and education.

All that advice is great, but what about getting started on the implementation? Help is at hand, towards the end of the book, in the third section, with a guide to planning that'll take your breath away, it's really that easy.

Features to look out for

That's the basic structure, but we've also included a number of features that come up from time to time, which are explained below.

'According to...'

We conducted a total of 21 in-depth interviews to get a wide range of input and opinion about the elements of effective communication and throughout the book you'll find quotes taken from those interviews that support what we're saying.

Apart from top business leaders and academics, we looked at communication in other spheres such as medicine and politics to see if the challenges were greater and if we could learn something that would adapt to our workplace.

A full list of the contributors can be found in Appendix II.

The expert panel

In addition to the short quotes that you find under the title of 'According to...' there are some more fully developed stories that stand alone. These you'll find in separate panels of text, interwoven with the rest of the book.

Try this

Having a go at something new can be a great way of refreshing our outlook on a subject. There are lots of practical suggestions of things you can do to make your communication better. It's up to you how many, if any, you do, but don't be afraid to think up your own new experiences.

A good story

Every now and again you hear a tale that perfectly illustrates a business situation you've been in. Sometimes they're things that really happened and sometimes made-up fables with a relevance to the problems we face. A collection of both kinds is contained in here; we don't expect you to believe them all, but hope that they'll amuse you and help you remember the vital points that they make.

The elevator test

Top firms of consultants use this technique when they're working with their clients. They prepare themselves to report succinctly on progress at any time by imagining they're caught in the elevator by the CEO and they have just a few floors to summarize where they're up to. We've applied a similar test at the end of each chapter to précis its contents.

Hopefully you're now about ready to get started, but before you do we thought we'd share what we learnt when writing this. We learnt the truth about honesty, who lies, when and why, about how 'charisma' is overused and indefinable, the real traits that great communicators have, the important things we've forgotten about communication (since we reached adulthood), including the marvellous gift of storytelling, and the bad news about some communication challenges. These are our revelations.

Part 1

Insight

What we discovered in writing this book and
what you can discover about yourself

1

Revelations

The truth about... the truth

Right from the start the truth was really important to us. Partly because our parents brought us up to believe it was the right thing, but also because we believe passionately that everyone's getting tired of the corporate-speak that seems to have taken over so many organizations.

Good business practice relies on trust, and what is that without truth? We set out to get to the bottom of what the truth is. It wasn't always easy.

Out of all the people we spoke to, there wasn't a single individual who advocated lying as a way to get on in business or personal life.

What was interesting was the range of views about what constitutes the truth – it seems that getting the definitive version of the facts can sometimes be more complex than you might think.

Here are the views of a number of contributors to give you a balance of opinion to compare with your own.

We start, not in the world of business, but in medicine, with Doug Simkiss, a Consultant Paediatrician at the Birmingham Community Children's Centre:

> At diagnosis I don't hide behind terms like a growth or a nodule or something, if it's cancer, it's cancer, if it's cerebral palsy, it's cerebral palsy – I use the medical term because if

you try and spare people the medical terms, they can't find any information afterwards, and anyway, if you don't use the proper terms someone else will, at some stage.

When it comes to the *whole* truth, in terms of the medical consequences of a condition, we're rubbish working that out at diagnosis anyway, because children are all different.

You can use the same terms about a child, like cerebral palsy for example, but the consequences can vary greatly.

So I guess I'd say we have to tell the truth as far as we know it, but the consequences become clearer over time and there often has to be a re-adjustment of what the truth means.

Telling the truth, as we know it, is very important, but even with the best of intentions it might not be possible to explain the whole truth. There are even times when the whole truth might be commercially sensitive or plain tactless, or you may encounter circumstances where people simply don't want to hear the truth, like in a redundancy situation.

Equally, the truth can be different according to where you're viewing it from. This is never more so than when two parties can't seem to compromise.

According to...

John Akers – Manager of National Family Mediation Service (Birmingham) and Relate Counsellor (Marriage Guidance)

In Birmingham there's a telephone tower which we could see from our offices – so I used to say to people if you look at that tower from here you know exactly what it looks like, but if you look at it from somewhere else in Birmingham it's different, because there are different satellite dishes you can see, but it's still the same telephone tower.

And, in the same way, your perception of this situation that you're in now is different, because you are only looking at it from one place – the truth is we have a problem here, but what the *facts* are is very much harder to find out because it depends on which position you are viewing from.

So the truth may be partly defined by the angle you view it from; more than this, our next contributor believes that the truth is contextual, that's to say it is of its time and place.

Background

In the 1980s, Britain's political scene was dominated by the Conservative Party, under Margaret Thatcher. In a move against this, voters in Liverpool elected Derek Hatton as deputy leader of the council.

Hatton was not only a member of the Labour Party but also belonged to the leftwing Militant faction, which eventually brought him into dispute with his own party members as well as the ruling Conservatives.

According to...

Derek Hatton – broadcaster and former Labour politician

> People often say to me, if you had your time over again would you do the same thing and I say if it was 4 May 1983, the day we took control, I wouldn't do a single effing thing different, if it was 4 May 2003 I wouldn't do a single thing the same.
>
> It's not about truth, it's about what is relevant at that time, and at that time, there needed to be a passion, there needed to be an understanding of what was going on, there needed to be support around, you needed to know how to motivate that support, you needed to know how to mobilize that support, you needed to be absolutely committed to what you were saying, it was not a case of truth or non-truth, you can play games with that if you want, but it's really about context.

If you're part of an organization that talks about truth and honesty, you have to make sure that they deliver across the board, not just in the glossy brochures that go to the outside world. There's currently lots of talk around about the 'employee brand', that is, the side of the company that the staff see. Most experts agree that what happens 'below stairs', as it were, has to be consistent with the customer view of the organization.

According to...

Lynn Rutter – Change Manager, Global HR Projects, Oxfam

> A lot of organizations haven't caught onto the need for honesty, they do this great external PR, put a lot of time and money into their advertising style and their brand image, and then on day one, the person starts and thinks 'hang on a minute, this isn't what I thought, where's the company I joined?'

In recent years, many large organizations have started to debate this issue by looking at the employee brand of the organization. What this means is that the workforce inside a company has a view of the values of the organization and increasingly the evidence points to a need to make this employee brand consistent with the consumer brand. So if your customers see you as standing for high ethical values, you must treat staff in a way that is consistent with this.

So, what can we conclude about the truth? We have a medical man who thinks that it can vary according to individual circumstance and a counsellor who believes that the angle of view changes the perspective. All of which is reinforced by the ex-politician who says that timing and context are paramount, and a business leader who thinks that consistency is the key.

The important learning is that however you look at it, the truth matters.

Getting the balance right

Honesty is a key plank of effective communication, but presenting a warts-and-all view of yourself at every opportunity is unlikely to endear you to everyone.

The most famous case of foot-in-mouth disease was that of jewellery tycoon Gerald Ratner, whose stores were once a feature of British high streets. In 1991 he made a speech to the Institute of Directors and joked that one of his firm's products was 'total crap', going on to boast that some of their earrings were 'cheaper than a prawn sandwich'.

The media instantly picked up on the story and the company dropped in value by £500m.

According to...

Keith Harris – Chairman, Seymour Pierce Group plc and former Chairman of the Football League

> Forget about the damage to the business, it was really about individuals who'd saved up to buy something from his shop, to give to somebody with all their heart and that was the real damage – that was truly awful.

The truth about... charisma

> *It's not all down to your natural personality because personalities don't change and I'm very clear that you can improve communication skills.*
>
> Chris Brewster – Professor of International Human Resource Management, South Bank University, London

The possibility that great communicators possess a mystical quality called 'charisma' is really quite scary. After all, if they have it and we don't, then how can we ever be truly great? In the spirit of busting some of the myths that surround communication we put this question under the microscope.

To the rescue came a number of authoritative figures who themselves excel in the art of communication. We start with a university professor.

According to...

Professor Chris Brewster

> I am extremely personally suspicious of words like charisma, first of all because I don't know what it means and, secondly, because you might look at someone and say they've got great charisma, and I'd say they look really boring, so unless we can have more certainty about judgements I think the whole concept is flawed.
>
> I don't dismiss the importance of other traits, like 'empathy' and a kind of understanding of where your audience is coming from.

We stay in the academic arena for another view that helps to reinforce what Chris Brewster thinks. David Clutterbuck is a Visiting Professor at Sheffield Hallam University.

The expert panel

David Clutterbuck – university professor

When it comes to charisma, I was told that originally it meant 'caring'. It seems to me to have the ability to project the fact that you care is really important – so all those words like passion are replaced by that.

We think, 'does this guy know what he's talking about, and does he care about the subject?' If you do then you'll get people's attention, but if either of those two things is missing then you won't.

I think that what you see as charisma is driven by those two things. There are people who are good actors, but mostly the people who communicate well are those who care and the passion that you see is just an external expression of what's going on inside them.

We did some work and found a number of organizations were concerned about the way people were appraised on their verbal communication skills.

It was the area where people most often disagreed with how they were appraised, so we did some focus groups (with Birkbeck College) and found the assumption that good verbal communication is just related to personality is bunk. It is, of course, partly related to that, but many other factors come in.

'Awareness of context' is fundamental, as is 'speed of communication'; for example, if you put a Finn and a Colombian together they're going to struggle, because one speaks very slowly and the other very quickly.

So the critical quality of a good communicator is the ability to adapt to the other person you're working with. Whatever the message, you have to structure it around the other person's ability to receive.

The really good news about charisma is that we don't have to try to seek it out as a holy grail, nor do we have to try to emulate the people who supposedly have it. In fact it may be that there are elements of it we can develop over time, according to our circumstances and status.

According to...

Derek Hatton – broadcaster and ex-politician

> David Beckham appears on television around the world with the most unbelievable amount of charisma, he's a working class kid, he's not the most articulate of blokes, there's nothing special about him but because of the way he's been built up, all of a sudden charisma oozes out of him. So I don't think it's necessarily what you've got, sometimes it's what other people give you.
>
> Okay, there are people that are born with it, there are people that naturally have it, they ooze that self-confidence and passion and everything that goes with it. I don't believe, however, that's the only form of charisma you can have, I think there are many forms of charisma that you can actually acquire, or other people can acquire for you.

In this section we've purposely tried to downplay the concept of charisma, but only because it seems to have developed an aura around it, a kind of saintly glow that makes it difficult to pin down.

If we can't define it properly, then it's going to be even harder to try to emulate it, better still to come up with a set of words that we can understand and aspire to. In our next section of revelations we try to do just that.

The truth about... great communication characteristics

It's all very well myth-busting, but if we say that charisma isn't all it's made out to be there must be other, more practical things we can look at, which form the basis of the personality of good and great communicators.

These are the traits we think are really important:

■ self-awareness
■ empathy
■ wit
■ passion
■ spark.

Now, here are a few words of explanation about each of those things.

Self-awareness

It's long been thought that the measure of ability in the form of IQ was a pretty poor way of summing up a person. We probably all knew the brainy kid at school who never went on to do much in later life. Alternatively, maybe the creative (but seemingly dumb) kid went on to be a great designer or had a gift for reaching autistic children.

Daniel Goleman (author of *Emotional Intelligence: Why it can matter more than IQ*, 1996) pioneered the measure of emotional intelligence, or EQ, and many have followed since, reinforcing the theory that part of what makes us capable individuals is how 'in touch' we are with our emotions.

A key part of this is our ability to look at ourselves and understand how the world sees us. How do our actions and emotions impact on the people we interact with? What response might we expect from them in return? Great communicators think about this all the time.

Empathy

This key ingredient will turn up as a running theme in the following pages. It's about being able to see the world through the eyes of your audience, even if on the surface you have nothing in common with them. If you can't see what they see you'll never be able to engage with them. Great communicators do this intuitively. Here's an example.

Charles is 52, and Managing Director of a large financial institution. His workforce is predominantly female aged 18 to 40. At the younger end of the spectrum are school leavers in their first junior role. The more mature workers include long-serving staff, many of whom are returning to work after maternity leave.

It would appear that Charles shares little common ground with either group, so how does he create empathy?

I listen.

As often as I can, I listen 'one to one' rather than in groups, and I try not to conclude that everyone is like this individual. However, the more 'one to one' listening I do, the more I can start to spot emerging trends. You have to see the whole person, not just the employee. We've offered cheaper mortgages to staff, helping the younger ones get on the first rung of the property ladder, and flexible hours to ease the problems of childcare for the mums. These are the issues that concern them, you have to understand that.

You don't have to be the same as the group you're trying to empathize with, but you do have to see *their* point of view.

Wit

We mean this in the widest sense of the word. It's not just about being funny (although that can be a big part of successful communication), but think of it also in terms of sayings like 'he had his wits about him', 'her response was very quick-witted'. In fact, wit is about having the ability to say or write things that are both amusing and clever, the ability to think quickly and clearly and make good decisions. And let's face it, there are times when we'd all like a bit more of that. Humour is without doubt a double-edged sword: use it well and you will display an incisive ability to drive your message home; badly, and you could end up scarred for life!

Passion

Just like sincerity, once you can fake it, you've got it made.

Actually, there is no replacement for passion and you can't manufacture it. Passion is driven by belief and faith; it's at our very core.

Think of something you feel passionate about, then imagine having to speak on the subject for a few minutes – how do you think you would look? How would you come across to your audience? If challenged on your beliefs, would you shrink back and concede? Or would you defend your position with vigour?

Now you can start to see how great communicators are able to inspire their audiences with the passion they feel for their subject.

Spark

First we ruled out 'charisma' as being too hard to pin down, now we're going to compromise by offering you 'spark' as an alternative. We're just trying to convey the look that some people have that sets them apart, that makes us want to get to know them. What adjectives do you think you'd use to describe someone with spark? Try these for starters:

- animated
- alive
- aware
- vibrant
- smiling
- enthusiastic
- lively
- energetic.

It may be that they have better, happier, more fulfilled lives than the rest of us, but it's more likely that they have simply developed a confidence in what they are saying, which comes across in the way that they say it, the way that they look and the way that they act.

Some personality traits will be inherited, but heredity is only part of the story; environment, the way we were brought up, our childhood experiences are all part of who we are now.

In the next section we look at what we might have forgotten since our childhood, and attempt to re-learn some of the things that made our lives much simpler then.

The truth about... children

Children are inclined to be direct, they don't beat about the bush, they're much more likely to say, 'I don't want this!'

John Akers – National Family Mediation Service

You don't just wake up one morning and think 'Hey! From today onwards I'm going to be a great communicator', well maybe you do, but you're fooling yourself. You have to plan and prepare yourself; you have to make time to be truly great.

You started acquiring your communication skills a long time ago though, in fact, you have already learnt a lot in getting to where you are now.

Sadly, you've forgotten a lot too and some of that would be really useful. Let's start by looking at what you might have to re-learn:

> I think children are more direct, more open and frank, and what can happen as we get older is that we behave according to the norms which may make us less direct and it's good to be reminded that direct communication is often the best, being frank, being succinct, being short and just telling it like it is.
>
> Val Gooding – CEO, BUPA

As adults we tend to take much more account of other people's feelings, we're sensitive to the environment we're operating in and aware of the subtleties of what is acceptable and what is not. Sometimes, though, this can work against us in achieving the things we want. In business, it can lead to an 'Emperor's new clothes' syndrome, particularly when the boss is aggressive and autocratic.

You reach a stage where everyone can see what's wrong but no one is prepared to question it. Being the little boy who stands up, points his finger and says, 'you're naked!' can be a liberating experience.

There is a health warning with all this, because sometimes you can liberate yourself right out of the organization altogether, so tread carefully and choose your moment!

According to...

Alistair Smith – founder of Alite Ltd and a leading expert on Accelerated Learning in schools

> There's certainly a lot that good communicators do that emulates what children do to learn naturally.

The research, whether into primates or the structure of the brain, points to certain natural ways of learning and includes things like 'imitation', 'safe rehearsal' without fear of recrimination and 'exploration', so you explore territory, you explore behaviours, you explore relationships.

The great thing about children is their 'openness', which allows them to do things like 'suspend politeness', and it's only when you suspend politeness that you can ask the disturbing question.

You'll get audiences with whom you're communicating, who will nod their heads and you'll think you're being very effective, but they'll leave you and go on doing and thinking what they were before and it's only when you've created relationships with them and asked the disturbing question that you'll make progress. Children do it habitually, and it's very powerful.

The other question children ask that good communicators ask is the 'so what?' question, 'This is all very well but what's it got to do with me? As a result of listening to you why am I better off?'

So for a communicator I think it's really important to acknowledge the significance of the 'so what?' question. It's a great sense check and it's the reason why in advertising they continually think about selling the benefits, rather than just talking about the facts.

Summary of what we've forgotten:

- Be direct and open.
- Keep it short.
- Ask the disturbing question.
- Ask 'so what?'
- Turn facts into benefits.

We've tended to concentrate in this section on the 'outbound communication' that we undertook as children, the 'what' and 'how' of letting others know our feelings. In the next section we move on to look at how we handled the information coming into us, how we learnt.

The truth about... storytelling

The best stories are universal and really skilled storytellers have the ability to embed their message.

Alistair Smith – Alite

The significance of storytelling is being recognized more and more in business. Or maybe it's simply being rediscovered after a time in the wilderness.

It's been easy over recent years to concentrate our thinking about communication around the 'channels of delivery', the technology if you like. We've all sat back and marvelled at the latest invention, the degree to which electronic memory has fallen in price, the growth of mobile phone ownership, the proliferation of television channels, the list goes on.

In that environment, we may have forgotten some of the simpler things in life that have had and always will have a massive impact on what we teach and learn, irrespective of how the messages are sent from one party to the other.

One of the key elements of our learning is 'storytelling'. When we're very young, it's one of the primary ways we find out about the world, about what's right and wrong and about our role in society.

The expert panel

Alistair Smith – education specialist

Every culture, every civilization expresses itself through stories, and stories are metaphors for how we live our lives, what should be of significance and value in our lives. It's how one generation translates its wisdom to another.

A thousand years ago, it was camp fire stuff and I guess the story tellers back then were as skilled at holding the attention, creating characters, embedding the learning points, activating the significant learning later and giving you a sense of closure when it was all done.

As for the media, well, they're just electronic stories.

Getting the people you work with to remember a certain point can be effectively executed through good storytelling, but raising the profile of a particular issue to a wider audience can also happen much more effectively if you have the right story, indeed if it's interesting enough, it'll even attract media coverage. Isn't this at the heart of public relations?

Here's a real-life example to illustrate the point. This story comes from the BBC's Head of Internal Communications, Russell Grossman.

The expert panel

Russell Grossman – BBC

I try to find particular examples and stories that people can relate to personally. So, for example, we wanted to get across the idea that 'bullying' is not acceptable at the BBC. It can be a problem especially in News and Current Affairs where it partly comes with the territory, because there are hard pressure deadlines and many people who are hard bitten.

If you go into a newsroom, you often have people shouting at each other: shouting instructions. If it doesn't get done on time they can feel verbally abused – that's not on. It's not confined to News, however, and also happens in wider programme making.

The best way for us to get this across was to tell a story by a person who was most involved with it. So we got somebody who was quite happy to say 'I'm the result of what we call BAFTA bastards, that's somebody who is recognized as great by the industry because they get a BAFTA, but actually back in the office they're an absolute bastard.'

And the fact that we outed it that way meant that the story was also reported in *Broadcast* magazine, *The London Evening Standard* and *The Times*.

My point is that if we'd just said that bullying is no good, it just wouldn't have made the same impact.

The shock tactics in this story are part of what gives it its impact; add to that the memorable phrase 'BAFTA bastard', which conjures up an instant picture of the talented but difficult prima donna. The point is then both well made and memorable.

There may be other occasions when you're not trying to make it into the daily papers, but are attempting to make your point more memorable. The trick is to make the story relevant to the point you're trying to get across, something that illustrates it in a vivid way in people's minds.

According to...

Lynn Rutter – Oxfam

> There's no point in standing up and giving a presentation in a way that the people aren't going to understand and, let's face it, glorious PowerPoint slides have their limitations.
>
> If you can't keep their attention and you can't tell stories you'll struggle, so I learnt to tell stories and talk in a way that people could relate to – so yes, it is something that I work at all the time.
>
> They don't need to be stories that are related to work, they can be just 'life stories', and if you tell a few that make fun of yourself that helps too.
>
> So I try to think of funny stories that people will remember, so that they'll then remember the bigger point behind it.

In fact, Lynn Rutter is an excellent storyteller, so you can look forward to one of her tales that turns up later in the chapter on culture and environment (Chapter 10).

Try this: *Start to collect stories*

When you hear a great tale, make a note of it and try to think through what it was that you liked about it. What 'learning points' was it making, can you re-apply that to a situation you'd like to teach to others?

Stories are often most powerful when they are about the person who is relating them, so think if you've been in a similar situation to the one in the tale. Don't stretch the truth too much and remember that it is sometimes better to credit the original storyteller.

What are the funny things that happen to you? Have you ever locked yourself out? Lost your car in a large car park? Made a terrible social gaffe?

What did you learn from that experience, and can you relate it to something you'd like others to know?

What's so good about 'stories'? Here's a reminder:

■ a great way to illustrate a point;
■ often common across all cultures;
■ high impact – very memorable;
■ a trigger for more serious learning;
■ good way of building rapport.

Some of the childhood experiences of the last couple of sections, the directness of approach and learning through stories are part of what makes you the person you are today.

To build on that you need to know yourself better, which is why we've got some exercises coming up to help you find out what you're really like as a communicator and how you rank in the great scheme of things. Before that though, a final revelation – it's not all good news.

The truth about... communication problems

Most people can do most things if they put their minds to it, it's just about believing.

Derek Hatton – broadcaster and ex-politician

That's a quote worth remembering when you come up against the inevitable communication problems you'll encounter.

At the start of the book we looked at the things that make great communicators, and how our growth through childhood into adults affects the way we relate to each other. Next you'll have a chance to look at the individual challenges that you face, then we'll move into looking at the practical things you can do to improve your own communication.

But before we get there it's only fair to say that all challenges can't be overcome that easily. Here's a final warning about some of the tough things you'll have to deal with.

The bottom line is that there are some messages people don't want to hear and, under those circumstances, it's very difficult, if not impossible, to connect with them.

According to...

Professor David Clutterbuck

> If people don't like the message they tend to ignore it.
>
> I recall one factory where they did just about everything they could think of to hint that the place was going to close, even to the point of measuring up the floor. When it was finally announced, the workforce went on strike, saying we didn't have a clue – people only hear messages that they are attuned to and want to hear.
>
> If a message is unpalatable, we tend to tune it out, and people's receptivity is affected by all sorts of factors. It can be about state of mind, about willingness to accept a message; it can be their perception of the person providing the data – if it comes from a source you don't believe to be credible, then you will probably be unreceptive, you won't take it in, especially if the message is contradictory to the basic judgements you have made about that individual or that organization.

This view is supported by Derek Hatton, a militant political leader of 1980s' Britain, whose views were directly opposed to the Prime Minister of the day Margaret Thatcher.

According to...

Derek Hatton – broadcaster and ex-politician

> I could say that someone like Margaret Thatcher was a good communicator, but that would be very difficult. The times that I met her I found she was a crap communicator because she was saying exactly the opposite of what I wanted to hear, and I suppose she would have said I was a crap communicator because I was saying exactly the opposite of what she wanted to hear.

One of the more difficult aspects of managing people is that sometimes you have to be the bearer of bad tidings. If they aren't receptive to that, then it will always be tough.

How to break the bad news

Being hesitant or vague, not coming straight to the point or dressing the message up in some way can just make matters worse. These are the times when you simply have to tell it like it is.

For an expert view on the best way of doing this we asked Consultant Paediatrician Doug Simkiss to talk about his golden rules for delivering bad news, bearing in mind this can sometimes mean telling parents that their children have a serious or critical medical condition.

The expert panel

Doug Simkiss – consultant paediatrician

I always make sure I can tell both parents together, and that I'll have enough time, free of interruptions, to both talk and listen.

After that I do my best to work out where they are and what their understanding of the current predicament is, and finally, I try to balance ruthless honesty with a sense of compassion.

People respond to integrity, and if the story is straight, I find that really helps to establish relationships, because sometimes these relationships are going to go on for 10 or 15 years, so it's important to reach a mutual understanding and respect for each other.

You have to ensure that people have plenty of opportunity to ask questions on the day, and you agree a date for a very early review where you'll sit down face to face again.

In a business situation (where whatever news you're delivering is not a matter of life and death), there are things that Doug Simkiss does that can be applied:

- If it affects a group of people try to tell them together.
- Allow enough time.
- Ensure there is an opportunity to talk and listen.
- Expect to have to answer questions.
- Try to find out what, if anything, their current understanding is.
- Be honest – make sure you have your story straight.

During the course of our interview with Doug Simkiss he also added that a colleague has started to make cassette recordings of some of these difficult consultations, so that the sometimes shell-shocked recipients of the bad news can later listen carefully to what has been said. It would be a good idea at least to have some accompanying written notes or answers to frequently asked questions to take away.

Setting a formal time for a further review meeting and making clear what your availability is in the meantime can also help the process.

That concludes our chapter on revelations, the things we learnt during the process of writing this book. There's plenty more learning to come, which we hope will help you become a better communicator, but first of all it's time to take a good hard look at yourself.

The elevator test for Chapter 1

The truth is important – be careful how you use it.

Sometimes, how much honesty you employ is affected by timing.

The term 'charisma' is subjective – it's related to caring, empathy, spark and wit.

Passion is a critical element of all truly effective communication.

Remember your childhood and be direct, open and frank – appropriate to the culture you're working in.

Storytelling is effective, the more so when it's relevant, personal and witty.

Storytelling helps embed important messages in the memory of your audience.

2

What kind of communicator are you?

The truth about... your individual style

Before you undertake the task of assessing your own communication style, have a look at the types we've defined below. How many of them do you recognize? Do you fit into any of these categories, or do you display some of the characteristics of more than one? There is good and bad in each, so try to capitalize on the positive aspects of the character types and steer clear of their shortcomings.

Try to think of at least one person you know who fits each description:

- **The secret agent.** Plays their cards close to their chest (too close sometimes). Treats the most insignificant of facts as confidential, especially if a superior has entrusted them with it. Good news: Reliable, discreet, trustworthy. Bad news: Staff confusion, breeds a suspicion culture, can be guilty of starting rumours.
- **The double agent.** Feigns discretion, but has a foot in another camp – may sometimes be on your side, but you'll never be sure (until you feel the knife in your back!). Good

news: Is a useful ally in the short term, especially in competitive environments. Bad news: Is likely to be judged as untrustworthy in the long term, and quickly becomes dispensable.

■ **The gossip columnist.** Collects tittle-tattle, or when all else fails makes it up. Believes the definition of confidentiality is 'tell one other person'. Good news: Has lots of 'friends', as everyone is willing to take the time to listen to the latest bit of scandal. Bad news: Lacks credibility and is unlikely to be trusted by colleagues.

■ **The dictator.** Listens to no one, makes snap judgements and decisions and tells it like it is or how they believe it is. Good news: Extremely clear in terms of direction and focus. Bad news: Resentment builds when people think their views aren't being listened to.

■ **The kitchen sink.** Tells everyone everything, even if it's not relevant to the topic in hand. Good news: Can never be accused of not keeping people informed. Bad news: Bores people to death, no focus on the task in hand, wastes vast amounts of time going round the houses.

■ **The mouse.** Has an opinion on many important issues but lacks the self-confidence or ability to express it. Good news: Astute, knows what is going on, may be seen as a good sounding board by others. Bad news: Lacks the ability to influence because of fear of speaking their mind.

Now try to get a measure of how effective your communication is by taking 10 minutes to answer the following questions.

Self-assessment – just how good a communicator are you?

1. When another person is talking to you, you tend to:
   a devote your entire attention to them;
   b listen to them but your minds wanders from time to time;
   c rarely listen with mind wandering a great deal.

2. When presenting a case, you tend to:
   a ensure that the people listening are given ample opportunity to intervene during your presentation;
   b sometimes allow people to intervene when you notice they want to;
   c like to finish before taking any questions or clarifications.

3. In trying to convince somebody to do something, you tend to:
   a present only rational arguments;
   b present rational arguments but use some emotional messages;
   c appeal to them on an emotional level.

4. Before communicating an important message to people at work, you tend to:
   a plan thoroughly what you are going to say;
   b think through what you are going to say but not plan it precisely;
   c do little planning, go with the flow and communicate in the here-and-now.

5. If somebody had not performed well on a particular job and you were the boss, would you:
   a be fairly assertive and direct about their performance;
   b try to communicate the problem calmly but also with some assertiveness;
   c try to support the person and let them know what they did that was wrong.

6. If you had to sack some people at work would you:
   a let the personnel officer do it;
   b leave most of the responsibility with personnel but offer the opportunity for discussion with yourself;
   c see each of them face to face.

7. When you arrive at work do you tend to:
   a plan all your communications by listing the meetings, e-mails and calls you need to make;
   b respond to what comes in throughout the day;
   c do some planning but build in a contingency for unexpected incoming tasks.

8. Do you view text messaging as:
   a a way of keeping in touch with friends to make social arrangements;
   b the primary method of keeping your colleagues updated;
   c a way of alerting workmates to important news.

9. Do you think the use of good spelling and grammar is:
   a a must-have tool in the communications mix;
   b an outdated concept as communication is now less formal;
   c nice-to-have, but not essential.

10. In important decision-making meetings do you tend to:
    a talk more than you listen;
    b listen more than you talk;
    c do both in equal measure.

How did you score?

Question 1   a = 3, b = 2, c = 1
Question 2   a = 2, b = 3, c = 1
Question 3   a = 1, b = 3, c = 2
Question 4   a = 3, b = 2, c = 1
Question 5   a = 2, b = 3, c = 1
Question 6   a = 1, b = 2, c = 3
Question 7   a = 2, b = 1, c = 3
Question 8   a = 2, b = 1, c = 3
Question 9   a = 3, b = 1, c = 2
Question 10   a = 1, b = 3, c = 2

What your score means
21–30
You are already a good communicator, thoughtful, passionate and prepared to listen. You take time to consider how the other party is feeling and are committed to continually improving your communication, both in terms of its style, and your command of new technologies.

You may sometimes find it hard to balance your IQ (intelligence) with your EQ (emotions) in choosing whether to present bare facts or the passion you feel about the subject.

11–20

You have a good instinct for communication, which will serve you well in most business situations. Most of the time you are fairly well planned, take time to think about what you are portraying to others, and are assertive in your actions.

Occasionally you may feel you have not presented your best side, or may have failed to justify your arguments because you have not had sufficient time to think them through.

1–10

Although you understand the basics of communication you need to take some time fine-tuning your style. You feel there are too many occasions when other people don't seem to understand your point, or take up a contrary stance for no good reason.

You may often get bogged down with information overload and need to find ways of filtering incoming messages to free up more time.

It might be that you are not making the best use of the available technology and could do with brushing up on tools and techniques.

Where are you now?

Our next exercise is designed to heighten your self-awareness, by asking you to take a good hard look at the kind of impression you currently make on other people, especially at a first meeting.

Choose one adjective from the three columns opposite that best describes how you believe other people see you.

Now think of where you would like to be. Consider this in terms of a person who might have impressed you on first meeting. What was it about him or her that gave you the 'wow' factor? Was it their position, the way they looked, a confident handshake, wit, a self-deprecating air, charm, what they said or the way that they said it?

SOCIAL SKILL	BUSINESS SKILL	ATTITUDE
Warm	Efficient	A doer
Outgoing	Demanding	A thinker
Engaging	Scatty	Aggressive
Witty	Smart	Submissive
Cold	Energetic	Cool
Stand-offish	Focused	Approachable
Shy	Rigorous	Empathetic
Measured	Effective	Understanding
Extrovert	Demanding	Pragmatic
Gregarious	Creative	Friendly
Reserved	Fastidious	Weak
Friendly	Decisive	Familiar
Cautious	Active	Collaborative

One stage further

As it is, this exercise is a useful way of working out the kind of communicator you are – if, however, you want an even more objective view, show the list to a couple of your peers and ask them to pick the three words they think sum you up best. The truth will probably be a mix of all the results.

Where do you want to be?

This exercise is designed to flesh out your existing perception.

Look at the 'word pool' below and answer both questions separately, by selecting just five words from the pool. You can have as much or as little cross-over between your two lists as you want, but be as honest as you can. It's much easier if you start by picking all the words in the pool that apply to each answer, and then filter it down to your final five.

1. How do you see yourself?
2. What other characteristics would you most like have?

The word pool

professional,
caring, self-reliant, tough, honest, effective, efficient,
tenacious, uncompromising, loyal, aggressive, creative, talented,
knowledgeable, serious, outgoing, popular, determined, visionary, shy,
amusing, cerebral, diligent, fastidious, industrious, helpful, conscientious,
faithful, hard-working, ambitious, humorous, easy-going, credible,
deep, intelligent, far-sighted, empathetic

There are two interesting aspects to this exercise. The first is in what we choose to describe ourselves, bearing in mind that initially we may have come up with 15 or 20 words; the need to prioritize helps to focus our attention on what we believe to be really important. The second factor is the transfer of words in and out of the pool, as the second question is answered.

At the end of this process you will have five words that describe how you want to be perceived in future and the kind of value system you wish to project.

What you have now done is to raise your level of consciousness about who you are and how you want to be perceived. The implementation of this in a variety of communication situations is easy, as long as you keep these adjectives in mind.

The truth about... how you compare

Great communication is a question of confidence. Often our outward appearance can mask our inner feelings.

Andy's presentation

Andy had just been promoted and had to give his first presentation to the senior management team. He prepared well, rehearsing the material frequently. A colleague had even gone through his PowerPoint slides with him as a double check. On the day, he delivered the presentation very well and afterwards his boss, who had been in the audience, took him to one side to congratulate him.

Andy confessed, 'I was really nervous' at which his boss surprised him and said 'Well, if that's true you hid it very well, it didn't show at all.'

This sort of conversation happens all the time and the important thing to learn is that often it's not how you feel inside, but how you project that is important.

Now you've completed the self-assessment exercises you may be starting to think consciously about your own self-confidence, just how good are you?

The great secret of business (and life in general)

Whatever you think about your ability, it is almost certainly at a lower level than other people view you.

A performance appraisal used to be something that was conducted by your manager, giving them the chance to tell you what they thought of you. Now more and more organizations are using 360-degree feedback where a much wider circle of people gets to comment on how you perform. This will probably include your peers, your customers, your staff and yourself.

Without fail you will mark yourself lower than anyone else does because for some reason many of us often think we're not as good as other people see us.

This doesn't mean you have no faith in your own ability, you probably know the things you're good at, but still we can scarcely believe that other people see us as so capable.

This feeling is no respecter of rank, status, age or experience. In researching this book, we found leading academics who'd quiver at the sight of a microphone pointed in their direction, articulate and inspirational business leaders who miraculously became tongue-tied when they knew we were recording the conversation.

It is our experience that everyone, regardless of status or authority, has some degree of self-doubt, some moment when they can't actually believe they've reached the position they now hold. If you look up enviously at some of these figures then take heart.

According to...

Cary Cooper – Professor of Organizational Psychology, UMIST

> I should actually listen to broadcasts I make, but you know why I don't do it, I'm frightened that I'll hear that I'm not very good and undermine my self-confidence, isn't that the stupidest thing?
>
> But it's an act of avoidance and I shouldn't do that really – I should listen to my radio broadcasts, watch my TV broadcasts and just see if I said silly things and what I can learn, but I'm frightened I'll think I'm so lousy, I won't go on again.

So, even leading academics have the odd crisis of confidence, but what about our most talented business leaders?

According to...

Simon Terrington – founding director of Human Capital, a consultancy that advises media companies on their creative strategies

> The thing is we're all just blagging it, aren't we? That's the whole point in life.
>
> You know that the syndrome that most chief executives suffer from is called the 'Outsider Syndrome', which is the fear that someone is going to tap you on the shoulder and say you've been found out, we know you've been bluffing the whole time, we know that you shouldn't really be doing this, you're not up to it. And everyone's afraid of that.
>
> I think we have a culture of hero worship, because we believe that chief executives are these supermen who create empires. I always think that in any company no one knows all the answers, and once you realize that, it's actually very liberating.

In the small hours of the morning, we can all lie awake worrying. At that time, none of us believes we are much good, but remember, it's what other people see that matters.

The truth about... how to get feedback

Getting feedback on a regular basis about the way we appear to others is a vital part of self-development; really effective communicators do this all the time and it's not difficult to achieve.

The easiest way to find out is to ask. You don't have to make it look like you're fishing for compliments or unsure of your ground either. If it's a colleague, a peer or even one of your own staff, you can ask in an open and honest way, and you will usually get a frank and honest answer.

It's here that a 'mentor', either officially appointed or unofficially adopted, can be a great help. The best thing to do is to find someone of a similar level within the organization who does a different job but understands your role – under these circumstances you can agree to a reciprocal mentoring deal, using each other to bounce ideas off.

You can also involve others on an occasional basis, so that you get a range of responses. For example, after a team briefing you might take one of your staff to one side and ask, 'How do you think the rest of the team will have received that information? Do you think what we're doing is clear? Is it fair? What problems do you think we might encounter?' They're sure to appreciate your honesty and feel good about you valuing their opinion.

Choose someone for your feedback whom you trust – it also helps if they have a degree of sensitivity because some of the things they tell you will inevitably feel uncomfortable at first, but it's honesty you want, not verbal abuse.

Raising your level of consciousness about feedback can also help, as in a range of situations, from one-to-one meetings through to formal presentations, you can start to observe your audience more critically for non-verbal signs of approval, or otherwise. There's a further section on non-verbal signals coming up later (see Chapter 10).

According to...

Val Gooding – BUPA

> One vitally important piece of advice I'd offer is to ask more
> questions – it works in a huge range of situations, maybe
> you're in a situation where you've been promoted to a new

job and you're not sure what you should be doing, a lot of people will try and cover up that they're not sure what they should be doing and swan around looking supremely self-confident. The best thing to do is ask questions whatever level you're at – ask questions, be nosy, be curious and don't be deterred if you're asking a question of a very senior person, somebody more important than you – keep asking questions, that's how you learn and become more effective.

Try this

Buy a Dictaphone. In the 1970s Dictaphones became popular as a way of replacing the conventional skills of the secretary. Because of this new technology you could sit and compose your correspondence at leisure, certain in the knowledge that the copy-typist would shape your ramblings into something resembling English.

Now these portable devices have a multitude of business uses. Handheld personal Dictaphones are about the size of a mobile phone and cost from around £30 for a reasonable quality model.

You can use your Dictaphone to take notes on any subject at any time. Even on a car journey you can set the machine to record as you start out and let it capture your outpourings along the way. If you're an 'ideas person', you can capture your inspiration as you go.

If you have to make a speech or presentation you can dictate it and listen back until, through repetition, you have memorized it. An extra tip here is to look out for one of the cassette-based models; although slightly bulkier than their mini-cassette equivalents, you can play back at home or on your in-car system.

When you need to get a more objective view of how well you're communicating, you can tape a meeting or presentation, and listen to your performance later. If you're lucky enough to have a mentor and brave enough to play it to them, the analysis is even more beneficial.

The elevator test for Chapter 2

Most of us are a mixture of different communication types – we adapt our style according to our surroundings.

Self-assessment exercises help us raise our consciousness – it's easier to see how other people view us.

We usually mark our own abilities below the level that others do.

Projecting confidence makes us look competent.

Seek feedback whenever possible – use a wide group of people and mix formal and casual methods.

Ask questions all the time – it's the best way to learn.

Part 2

How to...

The practical guide to much better communication

Introduction

The following eight chapters deal with the real practical issues of how to communicate effectively using a variety of tools across a range of situations. Because this forms a large part of the book, this introduction is a way of signposting the route ahead, to help you understand what to expect.

The 'how to' of great communication is easy as long as you stay conscious of the practical rules that govern it.

We begin at the beginning with a section on how to handle different communication channels when you're making contact for the first time, then we'll group communication into five main headings, reading, writing, listening, talking and feeling.

Within the writing chapters, we'll be discussing issues like use of plain language and how to persuade others to your point of view across a range of channels, including e-mail, text and Internet.

Then we'll look at talking and listening, where we cover the interactive face-to-face elements of communication that are such a big part of our working lives, so we look at meetings and presentations, and cover some of the current hardware that is commonly used, and misused, like voicemail and PowerPoint.

And we'll examine the non-verbal methods of communication that can signal so much, even on a subconscious level.

First though, here's a thumbnail sketch of some of the main methods of communication and how to use them.

'How to…' – Where to start?

We are continually forming relationships. Some are destined to be one-off events, appropriate to a single transfer of information; others are the start of something more significant. What they all have in common is the need to get things off on the right foot, and that is what this section is about.

On the phone

When you are about to speak to someone for the first time, avoid the urge to be impulsive, snatch up the receiver and dial the number.

Think first of all, about the *purpose* of the call. There's a very high likelihood that you'll be selling something. This is not in the literal sense, but more in terms of seeking to persuade the other party of something. You'd like them to attend a meeting or presentation; you need their input and advice on a project you're handling, that sort of thing.

The last thing that people want to hear is a lot of waffle, so jot down on a Post-It note the purpose of your call, why it is you've chosen that person in particular to speak to and any reasons that might motivate them to help you.

Contrast the two approaches below.

1. The ad hoc approach
'Hello, can I speak to Benjamin Allen please?'
  'Speaking.'
  'Oh hello Benjamin, my name's Sue Timson and I work at Hayes Autos, I don't know if this is your sort of thing or not, but they've asked me to ask you, so that's why I'm ringing. I don't know if you know Geoff Oxton, he didn't tell me if he knew you personally or if he'd just seen you speaking. Anyway he saw you last week when you were doing that thing about ethics in your organization at the Business Breakfast meeting in town, which is something we've been talking about for ages because our customers seem to be more conscious of it these days. So, would you consider, that's to say have you ever done this sort of thing for other companies

rather than as just a speech, like on a consultancy basis, not that we could pay much, but just as an adviser for an hour or two.'

2. The planned approach

'Hello, can I speak to Benjamin Allen please?'

'Speaking.'

'Benjamin, I'm calling from Hayes Autos. My colleague Geoff Oxton saw you speak on ethical trading at the Business Breakfast in town last week and thought you may be able to advise us on how to put a policy in place here. Is that something you think you could help with?'

The second example is businesslike, to the point, but friendly and open, which contrasts sharply with the unfocused nonsense of the first.

Face-to-face meetings

Think about what the meeting is for and who's going to be there, then, in your mind, fast-forward to after the meeting and think what you would like the other parties to be saying about you.

Were you self-assured or cocky?

Did you come across as thoughtful or lacking in any opinion?

Was your humour welcomed or winced at?

As you can see, for every positive outcome there is the risk of a negative. How assertive or quiet or amusing you attempt to be will be a matter of judgement on the day. If there is someone else at the meeting who's determined to hog the limelight, it may be better to back off and wait for the opportunity to state your case in a quiet, controlled and measured way.

To help you read these individual situations there's an in-depth section on non-verbal communication later on.

For the time being, here's an example of how you can prepare yourself for meetings, even if you've had little control over the parties involved and the agenda.

An important meeting

To help you develop a greater presence in any given situation, you can do a 'merit analysis' to raise your awareness of where you stand. This is nothing more complicated than listing the pluses and minuses of you as an individual when faced with this particular scenario.

Merit analysis case study

Nancy is a 28-year-old marketing assistant based in a regional office of a large stationery wholesaler. She has a meeting scheduled with the newly appointed marketing director from London, who is touring the regions getting to know the team. There are already signs that a plan is afoot to centralize all the marketing activity in London, something Nancy doesn't want to be a part of. No agenda has been set for the meeting.

This is Nancy's merit analysis:

▪ Positives
   - opportunity to set tone and agenda for meeting (build in contingencies according to how it is going – possible tour of plant, possible visit to top customer);
   - opportunity to discuss my past experience – draw up thumbnail resumé and practise delivery;
   - good knowledge of local marketplace;
   - good cost tracking in place;
   - evidence of regional initiatives helping win local customer loyalty and new business;
   - common ground – new marketing director used to work in food retailing – so did I (chance to build early rapport).

▪ Negatives
   - lack of control of budgets (set centrally already);
   - we don't get to see the big picture;
   - risk of presenting the company in a different way to other regions;
   - reduction in regional headcount may bring costs down (could be countered by the need to employ more people in London so costs might in fact rise);
   - communication issues with head office (what can we do to solve?)

You can see that as soon as Nancy starts to list the good and bad things about the situation she faces, a plan starts to form all by itself. This isn't a long-winded exercise; in fact, the above example took Nancy less than 15 minutes.

Don't make a meal of this kind of planning, but do set 'quiet time' aside well enough in advance to prepare the way – in Nancy's example she has to contact the operations manager to help clear the way for the tour and put a call in to the customer.

Action

Your one-to-one meeting is about to start, you've taken appearance and presence into account, you should be in a well-prepared state, confident of your ground, with some contingency planning to further bolster your position.

The final element is *action*, the things you do and say during the meeting. As communication is a two-way process, your actions will to a great extent be governed by how the other party behaves. In our example above, Nancy is meeting her manager for the first time – with experience we all get better at assessing the best way to handle different types of character.

Letter, e-mail or other written method

There are special circumstances you have to consider when sending a written piece of communication to someone you don't know. With the other two cases above (phone and face to face), you have some chance of judging how the meeting is going and how well your message is being received by the other party; in short, you can alter course a bit if it looks like it's not finding favour.

Obviously that's something you can't do if you've written to them, as you're not there when they read it. For this reason we urge greater caution; don't take risks with humour and unless you've got a very good reason not to, keep it short!

It's certainly true that in all the scenarios we've described here, you will rely heavily on experience and having your wits about you. What we have discussed, however, is a number of ways you can prepare yourself mentally in advance of these communications, rather than rushing, relying solely on your natural charm!

3

The truth about reading

Is this too simple for you?

After all, reading is such an everyday occurrence it's almost like having a chapter on how to breathe or how to walk. Yet, the importance of knowing what, how and when to read is greater than ever, as it remains one of the primary ways we receive information and form opinions about the world around us.

The concept of being well read is one that appeals to many of us, but achieving it can be a lifetime's work. It's about acquiring a knowledge of not just the classics, but of a wide range of other works across the whole spectrum of literature. Although the investment in time is great, the rewards are correspondingly rich, broadening our knowledge and our ability to communicate with others in an authoritative and entertaining way.

You can improve your own ability to communicate effectively by making your reading a conscious action, by being selective about what to read, when to and how to.

The truth about... what to read

You gotta look at everything you're supposed to read and put it into piles and say this is really important, this isn't so important, and that down there... I'm never going to read that!

Professor Cary Cooper

We're not here to extol the virtues of one newspaper over another, or compare and contrast a selection of trade magazines, because what you read is really up to you.

However, you may find the following criteria useful in making some conscious decisions:

- What do you need to know for work?
- What is the minimum expectation of what you know about your job and what extra knowledge would be regarded as added value?
- Where is your individual balance of interest between home news, national news and international news?
- How do you like to spend your free time?
- What do your friends talk about?
- When do you feel you're excluded from a discussion (because you don't know about the subject)?
- Who do you admire and what 'knowledge' do they have that you don't?

When you've answered these questions, you should be able to come to a view of where your 'reading gaps' are. It may be that you want to be more of an authority on some aspect of your work, in which case internal publications or trade magazines could be the best route.

On the other hand, it could be your general knowledge of the world at large that you want to improve (all of which impacts on our working lives in some fashion), and here, a quality newspaper or credible current affairs website will help.

Consider how many aspects of knowledge (BREADTH) you are going to cover and the amount of detail (DEPTH) you believe is desirable; this will be the key to governing the way you read.

According to...

Lynn Rutter – Oxfam

> The biggest advice I would give is that the world doesn't operate in a vacuum. When I joined British Telecom many years ago, you thought that all you had to do was understand the world of British Telecom and you'd get on in life.

But the people who were successful were the ones who stuck their head above the parapet and saw a world outside British Telecom. The ones that had spent 20- or 30-year careers only developing the skills of how to work the British Telecom process, found themselves completely lost when they were made redundant.

So my advice would be to set aside time to keep yourself informed; information will not be handed to you on a plate, you'll have to go and look for it. So attend meetings and presentations being held about the new product or whatever, even if it's not related to you or your job – take a broader view of what's going on and actively keep yourself informed. Secondly, look outside your own industry; don't assume if you work for Nokia, for example, that the only thing you need to keep up with is what's happening in other mobile phone companies – your best ideas often come from completely different industries that are nothing to do with what you're doing.

The truth about... how to read

We don't read everything in the same way. Think for a minute about the impact of an advertising hoarding on your consciousness, versus the level of knowledge you absorb from your bank statement. It is because the messages are designed with different outcomes in mind that our method of taking them in differs.

Environment is also an important factor here. The advertiser, who is trying to sell you something, knows you will only glance at the poster while travelling along in your car. On the other hand, the bank manager, who is attempting to keep you better informed about your personal finances, knows you will take at least some time, possibly in your office or at the kitchen table, to look in detail at the information.

We are constantly making these assessments of how important information is, without stopping to think about it. Because we return time and again to the theme of conscious communication, it's time to make some value judgements on how to read the different types of information that come your way.

You will, by this stage of your life, have developed an automatic reading style. People who read slowly tend to take every word individually and marvel at those who can skim swiftly through a passage, yet still retain the same amount of information from it.

It's hard to break away from your natural style but you should try to adapt the way you read according to the importance of the information being presented, increasing your level of 'absorption' for critical information, like this week's sales figures, and turning it down for more casual, leisure-based reading.

Try this

Most busy managers increasingly rely for their information on the 'executive summary', a page or two of headlines, presented at the front of a report. During one of your high-attention reading sessions try to distil the contents of the article into half a dozen bullet points, without losing any significant facts.

This is a useful exercise because it not only focuses your mind on what you've read, helping you to remember the really important points, but it also lets you practise writing this kind of summary, which you will find useful the next time you are asked to present your ideas on a particular topic.

In practice we need to increase the number of conscious assessments we make of what to read. Here's a real-life example to illustrate the point.

You turn up for an important job interview 10 minutes early and the receptionist asks you to take a seat. She has also been told to inform you that part of the interview will involve a discussion of a variety of current affairs topics.

A quality broadsheet newspaper is lying on the table in front of you. In the time allowed you could read the whole of the front page, or the headline and opening paragraph of at least two-thirds of the stories in the paper. What would you choose to do?

What you've seen so far in this section may have made you decide to read more; if so, you need to think about how you're going to fit it in.

The truth about... when to read

You need to consider two factors. Firstly, in terms of quantity, how much do you want to read? And secondly, what is your lifestyle like? Does it support your new strategy?

If this all sounds a bit too prescriptive then think back to some of your good intentions in the past and ask yourself what it was that got in the way of fulfilling your ambitions.

You might find that planning this kind of time is easier if you think in terms of two sorts of time-slots for reading, core time and bonus time.

Core time is set in stone; you choose it in advance and have it 'booked out' for whatever you've selected, so you could say 'I will take one hour every Sunday morning, between 10:30 and 11:30, to read my favourite newspaper.' Having a start and end time will also help you to focus how you read, as we discussed in the previous section.

Bonus time is the precious minutes you find yourself with unexpectedly, on the train, over breakfast, while waiting for a colleague to arrive.

In reality this even happens as a matter of course, after your core time has elapsed. Having discovered an item worthy of further investigation, you may choose to go beyond 11:30 or make time in the afternoon.

You can apply the same principle to the working week by resolving to set aside 15 minutes of core time every morning to catch up with the company newsletter or intranet site, or to read a relevant trade magazine.

If you're starting to think that living your life like this would drive you mad, remember this: firstly, you are doing this for yourself, to increase your knowledge and become better informed, and secondly, this core time/bonus time approach doesn't take up your whole life – you may only allocate a couple of hours a week to this activity (and incidentally, it should supplement your existing reading, not replace it). Finally, you should find some way of rewarding yourself for achieving your goal, which will increase your gratification in the experience. How about proper coffee and fresh croissants to complete the Sunday morning experience?

In summary

In this chapter we've acknowledged that reading is a critical element of communication, one of our primary methods of acquiring knowledge. Equally, we've recognized the amount of time it takes up and because this is such a finite commodity we need to make choices about what we read. That decision-making process can be helped by asking ourselves a few basic questions about what we're trying to achieve with our reading: is it to become more knowledgeable about a particular topic, to increase the breadth and depth of our conversations or to catch up with what's happening in the world of media and enter-tainment? No doubt it will be a mixture of these things and more, but by making some conscious decisions about what we read, we stand to gain more from the activity.

Staying on an objective and conscious level, you can start to take decisions about how to read different articles. An important report that you need to discuss with colleagues may require concentrated effort, including some note taking, as in our exec-utive summary exercise earlier. Alternatively, a look through the entertainment guide to see what this week's movies are or catch up on the odd music review probably only requires a quick skim.

We finished by looking at the whole subject of when to read. This is supplementary reading over and above what you would naturally do and it's designed to make you better informed about your own choice of subjects.

We now live in a world that could be described as content-rich. Technology is increasing the availability and number of media streams, all of which we can use to absorb information and entertainment. What hasn't changed is our ability to read more than one article at a time.

Try this: *Online curiosity*

Pre-Internet, you had to make a conscious effort to exercise your curiosity; it may have meant a visit to the local library, or a bookshop to purchase a relevant text.

Now you can take 10 minutes a day to be better informed about an aspect of general knowledge that you haven't explored.

Find a search engine that you like and trust and make a list of all the things you might have been curious about in a fleeting way over the past few months. Think, too, about what makes the world go round; explore politics, religion, family values and culture, modern history, art and literature – there's a vast array of subjects that your online search will give you an insight into.

Best of all, you can consume as much or as little as you want at any one time, saving the sites of interest in your 'favourites'.

According to...

Professor Cary Cooper

> What managers do that is so wrong is to read whatever it is that hits their desk. They pick it up and start doing it.
>
> Very often managers will read an e-mail and deal with it there and then, regardless of its priority, and some of that is about avoidance.
>
> Sometimes there are certain things that they have to do which they hate, so they'll find any excuse to pick up anything from e-mail rather than have to do what they should be doing.

Choose carefully and always remember that reading should be a pleasure.

The elevator test for Chapter 3

Reading is critical to our absorption of FACTS to help us form OPINIONS.

We have too much to read – setting priorities is vital.

Think about what you NEED to know and WANT to learn – balance these factors to select what you read.

Always keep your selection criteria in mind; make conscious decisions.

Think of reading as a 'special' activity – set time aside for it.

Apply a level of ATTENTION to your reading that's appropriate to its level of IMPORTANCE.

4

The truth about writing

Words are like the loose change in your pocket, it's not how many you have, but their value that counts.

Anon

How to write

Well-crafted text is one of the most powerful persuaders in the whole spectrum of business communication and learning the techniques of good writing will turn out to be well worth it.

If you need convincing about the significance of the written word, then you should think about it in the following terms: when you send someone a piece of written communication they will receive two things, firstly, some raw data or information, and secondly, a means of making value judgements about you the sender.

It's not just what they read, but what they read *into* it that's important.

We're going to be exploring the different types of written communication that we commonly use and looking at the similarities and differences between them; we'll examine how to establish your own writing personality and when to adapt your style to fit the circumstances.

Perhaps most important of all, we'll analyse ways of using your writing as a means of persuasion in Chapter 5, with particular reference to the advertising industry.

The truth about... establishing your writing personality

In an earlier chapter, you went through the process of finding out what you are like by looking at the good and bad of a number of communication-types. This may leave you feeling relieved that you haven't adopted the worst traits of bad communicators and a bit envious of others who seem to have got it right.

At no stage would we advocate you undergo a personality makeover, but when it comes to the written word there's quite a lot you can do to improve the way you appear to others – we call this 'establishing your writing personality'.

According to...

Professor Chris Brewster

> I like the idea of a 'writing personality', and I definitely think you can develop an individual style as long as you remember to adapt to your audience.
>
> Even though I'm an academic now, I've benefited from being a journalist in the past because it helped me realize how to write in a very understandable way.
>
> I've tried to develop a style that's very plain and straight-forward, whereas some academics choose to speak in a way that some find difficult to understand.

Try this

You can become more conscious of the impression you make on people if you take time to analyse the writing personality of others.

Spend an hour in the library and pull out, at random, three or four books by authors you don't know. Dip into the middle of each and read a passage, then note down what you think the author is like – male or female, what age group, nationality, background.

Next, write down the reasons why you think this: is it use of language, the story itself, the tone of the piece? Then turn to the inside cover and read the official notes about the author to check how accurate you were.

This is a great way of gaining an understanding of how people read into what we've written.

What you say and the way you present your written work is something that reflects the kind of person you are, and in order to be seen in the best light you need to bring a higher level of consciousness to your written communication.

Look back at the word pool exercise you completed earlier and think about what people would expect of you. If it showed that you're a 'thoughtful intelligent person', then your written work should reflect that; if you came across as more 'laid back and creative', you need to take a different approach to signal that.

In thinking about your personality you need to get the balance of honesty right.

Think of your written communication like an advertisement placed in the personal column of a newspaper.

You'd expect to find people listing their best qualities and showing a fair degree of honesty; after all, if things progress any further and you meet up, a claim of Brad Pitt or Jennifer Lopez looks is likely to be exposed for what it is (unless of course you happen to be Brad Pitt or Jennifer Lopez).

Equally, describing yourself as middle aged, overweight and bald won't get you off first base, especially if you happen to be a woman.

Presenting things in their best light has become the currency of politics, now often called 'spin' – but there's a big difference between this and telling lies.

According to...

Peter Sanguinetti – Former Director of Corporate Communications, British Gas

> Spin has become part of our lives – the important thing is to determine whether it is a case of putting the facts across in the best possible manner or deliberately misleading people;

the latter is unethical, undesirable, ill advised and likely to lead to you being caught out and losing credibility.

The truth about... applying your writing personality

Knowing 'who' you are is important, but you also have to be conscious of how you present yourself. Many people fall into the trap of trying too hard to sound important, particularly if the circumstances of the communication are more formal.

These days we no longer have to try to impress other people with our command of big words or flowery language – Plain English is here to stay.

The benefits of Plain English

Look at the following example, which illustrates why Plain English is so important.

In real-life conversations no one uses words like 'herewith' or 'perusal', and yet they turn up in job application letters with alarming regularity. Instead of 'please find enclosed herewith my curriculum vitae for your perusal', try 'I've enclosed my career history for you to look at'.

These days, if you can't use Plain English well, you are likely to be judged as pompous and condescending. Even in the legal profession, well known for its use of elaborate language, things are changing.

David Harper is Head of the Employment Department at the leading law firm Lovells, and he believes the use of legalese (the old-fashioned language that some lawyers still use) is outdated. He has harsh words for those who still persist in using it and cites three key reasons why they might continue to do so:

■ Insecurity – if you really did know what you were talking about then you'd put it in simple terms rather than dressing it up to try to confuse your audience.

■ Arrogance – the belief that these issues are so complex and difficult for the layman to understand that they need their own specialist form of flowery language to describe them. This is usually misguided.

■ Uncertainty – a lack of clarity of thinking which results in using a very verbose style to try to mask the fact that you're not sure what you're talking about!

David Harper advocates a much simpler and down-to-earth approach to communication, which could be why Lovells have won a Plain English award.

The truth about… the basics of Plain English

The following hints and tips are designed to help you to write better Plain English. They can, and should, be used across all written media. Note also that these rules apply irrespective of your audience. Although it may be tempting to use longer words and more complicated phrases when you are writing to the boss (in an attempt to impress him/her), resist this impulse. They'll see through it and you'll just look daft.

First things first – whatever you're writing, you'll need to start with some form of heading or headline. Even e-mail allows you to do this, so make sure you always fill in the subject field. Stop and think what this achieves. If well written, your headline will grab the reader's attention and draw them into the body of the piece. You can adopt an approach that is either **factual** or **curious**, but be careful.

A **factual** heading is simply designed to be the shortest form of words you can find to sum up what the body text says. E-mail is a great discipline for practising this, as when it arrives in the recipient's inbox they will only be able to read the first half a dozen words or so within the subject field. This forces you to be extremely succinct, as in the next example.

Less is more

There are times when fewer words have significantly more power than many. This was certainly the case for one philosophy student who sat in an examination room with his fellow students. The question on the paper in front of them was 'What is a risk?'

A good story

While the rest of the students chewed their pencils, furrowed their brows and scribbled furiously, he calmly wrote his answer, stood up and walked out.

The curious adjudicator came to collect his paper.

On it was his two-word answer.

'This is.'

Curious headings include questions, puns or puzzles and they have the same objective of enticing the reader to want to know more. When it's executed well, this type of opening is extremely effective, but take care to deliver on your promises. That old technique of putting a headline like 'Free Beer!' and then going on to say 'Now that we've got your attention etc, etc' will simply annoy readers. This has been the downfall of much of the 'spam' e-mail we receive. We're now so used to the kind of attention-grabbing puff that accompanies this unwelcome intrusion into our inbox that most of us have given up on opening the e-mail itself, knowing that the 'promise' won't be fulfilled.

The truth about... how to write a good story

The BBC trains its journalists to shy away from putting too much detail in a headline; they recommend that the essence of the story should be summed up in four or five words, and on no account should it stretch over more than two lines.

Their golden rules are as follows:

■ Sell the story (but don't oversell it, as this can lead to disappointment).
■ Avoid jargon and clichés (using words like 'slammed' or 'blasted').
■ Avoid being too cryptic (and remember that all audiences won't be on the same wavelength).

Apart from having a beginning, middle and end, a good story relies on the application of some basic rules:

■ *Editing* – tautology is the practice of saying the same thing twice using different words, and it's a waste of time for both the author and the reader. Avoid repetition and use clean and efficient phrases to get your message across. When you've finished composing your piece, read it back and delete any unnecessary words. At the same time, you need to try to make sure you maintain the flow of the message. Busy people will soon come to appreciate that you are an effective communicator with clarity of thought.

■ *Sequence* – each paragraph should deal with a single theme. That is to say, it should start out with the core idea, be developed with a sentence or two and, towards the end, signal the expected subject matter of the next paragraph. Writing in this way allows you to order your individual paragraphs into a coherent story that flows in a logical sequence.

A further tip on structure is that you should consider the use of bullets and numbering. This kind of writing has become particularly important in writing web pages, as Internet users rarely have the time and patience to plough through large blocks of text. (There's a more detailed section on how to write for the Internet later on.)

■ *Style* – Active is much better than passive. What this means is that you should try to write in a way that puts the 'actor' before the action. Here's an example:

'The president has called for tough action on street crime.'

A passive way of saying the same thing would be as follows:

'Tough action is required on street crime according to the president.'

Active writing is much more dynamic and engaging for your audience.

Finally, when it comes to style, try to keep your sentences short. This allows the reader a much better chance to pick up the relevant facts quickly and easily.

It's not only in journalism that Plain English is important; all aspects of business benefit if we are prepared to simplify what we are saying. Read below the example of how the BBC started an initiative to dispense with waffle.

The expert panel

Russell Grossman – BBC

The cut-the-crap card was something we introduced in February 2002. Greg (Dyke, former Director General of the BBC) is a football aficionado, so we came up with the idea of a yellow card, like a referee would have, and put on it 'Cut the crap, make it happen'.

As part of explaining to managers how we wanted to encourage greater creativity and more collaborative working, Greg took out the card and said, 'I've had these special cut-the-crap cards made. Anybody that wants one can have one. So, if you're in a meeting and you feel that creativity is being stifled then wave this card.'

The device worked partly by using the word 'crap' which at least made people sit up and take notice – *The Independent* newspaper reported that it was the 27th most offensive word in the English language – but it also sent out the signal that we want to talk in Plain English.

So we say, for example, don't send a memo that says we will 'commence operations tomorrow', say 'we're going to begin work'; don't talk about 'implementing a project', talk about 'doing it'; don't talk about 'procuring something', talk about bleeding well 'buying it'!

Using the behavioural example of the cut-the-crap card we've found that people in the BBC both speak and write now in a more direct, informal, say-what-you-mean manner. As a result we have less frustration, a lesser sense of bureaucracy, and more general understanding of what people are saying.

For some people using Plain English doesn't come naturally; they may believe in the benefits of it, but it just doesn't seem to happen. Here's an example from a business leader who got it wrong:

> I think that a lot of the language of banking and financial services was very opaque, indigestible and inaccessible to ordinary people, and there's been a huge drive to increase the simplicity and the transparency of it.

It's just a very wordy way of talking about making things plainer!

The truth about… the context of the written word

When it comes to what is acceptable in a written format things change over time, so it's no real surprise when older colleagues start to lament the downfall of good grammar and mourn the passing of a generation who knew when to use a colon versus a semi-colon.

But we think that writing should be viewed in the same way as design or fashion; it's a thing of its time and it adapts to society's collective changes in attitude.

E-mail has had a big impact on that. No one sat down and wrote the rulebook for e-mail, and a good thing too. Instead it has evolved as a form or writing all of its own, halfway between a letter and a chat on the phone.

The outcome of all this is that written communication in all forms has become more informal and less bound by rules and regulations.

You might start to believe that anything goes – it doesn't.

The truth about… the basic rules of written English

Presentation

Just a generation ago the only people in the office who could properly present a piece of written work were the secretaries; now everyone can do it, thanks to well thought out, user-friendly word processing packages. The downside of this is that most people are self-taught when it comes to layout and presentation, with the result that you tend to see the full spectrum of styles, from the minimalist to the garish!

Many large organizations issue style guidelines, especially if the company's logo is to be incorporated into a document, and you may even find that there are recommended fonts and point sizes to be used on outgoing mail – it's certainly worth checking.

If no such guidance is available, here are a few tips to help you get the basics right.

You may think that the more ornate your document the more likely it is to be read. In most cases the reverse applies; after all, you don't want to distract the reader from the sparkling prose you've put together, and anyway, they are unlikely to see fancy presentation as a substitute for worthwhile content.

Think 'consistency' all the time. Changes in the size and type of font look sloppy and untidy, and it'll probably result in the reader thinking you simply couldn't be bothered to check it before it was sent.

Keep it simple; where you have chosen to use the format keys (bold, italic, etc) make sure there's a reason, like the signalling of a new subsection by an emboldened sub-heading. This will help to signpost the reader through your document and make it easier to understand and digest.

Use short sentences. If you take a leaf out of the advertising copywriter's book, you'll soon see how you can get points across more effectively by keeping your statements succinct. Contrary to popular belief, this doesn't make you appear any less intelligent than your more wordy colleagues, in fact the opposite often applies.

White space is the report-reader's dream. Most people, when faced with huge blocks of solid text, turn off immediately. Make sure you break up your document with plenty of gaps between paragraphs; lists of bullet points or diagrams and illustrations are equally useful in providing some light and shade.

Now to prove the point of the last paragraph here's a list of bullet points summarizing the presentation tips:

- Don't get fancy.
- Consistency, consistency, consistency.
- Keep it simple.
- Short sentences.
- Use white space.

Structure

The specific structure of your written work will depend on its primary aim – a report is rather different to an e-mail. All the same, there are some things you need to consider across the spectrum of your work, all of which are designed to make it easier for the reader and therefore more likely that they will accept what you're saying.

Before the reader gets into the main body of the piece, it's very helpful if you manage their expectation early on.

So, you might say: 'In three sections, this report outlines our current appraisal policy, the results of a recent staff survey on the issue and recommendations for change.'

Or when a call to action is required: 'I'm sending you this e-mail to get your input before Friday's meeting.'

In both cases the reader knows right from the start what to expect.

Usually you need to get the important information across first, so if you were writing a report, this might be in the form of an executive summary at the beginning. In more informal communication, like e-mail, you might simply summarize the detail in a list of bullet points near the start.

To finish, you should construct a short conclusion that summarizes the main points of the correspondence and the expected action.

Now that you've established a working structure for the document, you need to go back to the start and ensure that it follows a logical sequence. Ask yourself the question why each section follows the other and check to make sure that you haven't included any superfluous information – remember that further background reading can always be placed after the main body, like an appendix; the reader can then choose to delve deeper if they wish to.

Tone of voice

You may think it's unusual to talk about the written word in terms of tone of voice, but it is immensely important as a tool for bringing your writing to life. In the light of what we've seen earlier about the relationships we form through our communication, it's more important than ever that we pay attention to this kind of detail.

As you type onto your computer screen, there is a 'voice' in your head and the same applies when the document is read at the other end. It's a bit like those old movies where one character is reading a letter they've received and you hear the voice of the character who sent it.

Don't confuse this aspect of your writing with style; tone of voice is more about *mood*. When your message is read at the other end you want it to accurately reflect how you were feeling when you wrote it:

■ A thank you note to your staff should convey genuine gratitude.

■ A letter of complaint to a supplier needs to reflect the seriousness of the issue.

■ Requesting the opportunity to tender/pitch for a piece of business has to suggest legitimate professional interest.

■ A rallying call to your team should sound genuinely enthusiastic.

The truth about... spelling and grammar

If attitudes really are more relaxed than they used to be you could be fooled into believing that you don't need to pay too much attention to spelling and grammar. But think back to what we said earlier about how the recipient of your message will interpret it; not only are they forming a judgement about the communication itself, but also of the sender.

Spell-check software is now universally available, so when a document arrives with errors in it, even if it's only an e-mail, it doesn't tell the reader that you're stupid or didn't pay attention in English lessons at school; it sends the signal that they're not important enough for you to have read it through before sending it.

According to...

Kay Winsper – Head of Great Company, Microsoft

> If I receive something with a spelling mistake in, what do you think I concentrate on within that piece of communication?
> All the messaging is taken away by you being drawn to the things that are wrong, so I think it's imperative to spell

check, otherwise it just looks like you don't care, it looks sloppy.

Although spell check is a great invention, it only 'reads' what you've written; it can't read your mind. This means that words you misspell, which actually make other proper words, will not show up – to illustrate the point have a look at the following anecdote, told by a senior executive to his management team.

Always check your smelling

'I fully understand that my reputation is one of being a bit of a technophobe but you will all be pleased to know that I have attended an e-mail training course and have become fully conversant with all the functions available. May I offer you a word of caution, however, when using the spell-check facility?

'Last week I wrote to my head of finance expressing grave concern that we had a considerable "under spend" against a number of budget lines as we approached year-end. In a rush, I quickly spell checked the e-mail and hit the send button.

'She replied asking if I really meant what I'd said and when I re-read the document I discovered to my horror that I had written the following…

Dear Grace,

Please can you contact me urgently to arrange a meeting? It has come to my attention that I have a number of large under-pants, which could land us both in deep trouble…'

It doesn't matter if it's true or not, you get the point.

As far as the subject of grammar is concerned, you are better off relying on care and attention than the grammar check on your computer. The reason for this is that grammar is much more subjective than spelling, and although there are some hard and fast rules, there is often room for interpretation too.

Having the computer make suggestions for everything you write can change the sense that you were trying to convey. It's not that you shouldn't refer to the advice, but don't feel duty bound always to take it.

A good story

If you're committed to improving your writing style, there are lots of courses available at local colleges that will help, not just grammatically, but with creative input too. Alternatively, if you're part of a mentoring scheme set up by your employer it's an objective you could add to the mix.

How does it sound?

The carpenter's rule

Time-served craftsmen in any trade are hard to find and the old school tended to learn their skill in a painstaking way. Apart from the practicalities, this was often accompanied by short phrases and sayings to remind the apprentice of the golden rules.

Jacko, a carpenter from the old school, shared this piece of wisdom with us: 'measure twice, cut once'. It simply means you should check and double-check the length you want before committing the saw to the timber, as once you've done so there's no going back.

Apply the same double-check rule to every piece of written work you intend to send out and it will improve overnight.

Reading your written work back twice gives you the opportunity to look for spelling and grammar errors, but has the extra benefit of making sure that what you're saying sounds right. Is it in a logical order, well reasoned, clear and easy to understand? Will the recipient know right away what you are trying to communicate?

Here are a couple of extra tips for really important written communications. Firstly, if you're not convinced it sounds right then try reading aloud – if it sounds daft, it probably is. Secondly, if you want to get a much more objective perspective then print out what you've written – very often you'll find you see things differently on paper to on screen.

One last thing, does what you've written look polite? Have you treated the other party with a degree of respect?

Here's a list of the things you should never do when you're writing:

■ Never be afraid to use a dictionary or thesaurus (there are some great ones online).

- Never send any written communication without reading it to yourself at least once.
- Never spell the name of the recipient wrongly.
- Never fail to check your spelling – before computers were invented, misspelled words were a sign of poor education; now, with the availability of spell checkers, they're a sign that you don't care!
- Never abandon your natural style and try to look clever – if you are clever it will show anyway.
- Never waffle.
- Never forget to whom and why you are sending this.
- Never allow ambiguity to creep in.

According to...

Jan Shawe – Director of Corporate Communications, Sainsbury's Supermarkets Limited

> Call me old fashioned but I think good grammar is important. I think particularly these days when a lot of senior people are doing their own e-mails and they probably weren't trained as shorthand typists there's the chance that they won't type as well as a trained typist.
>
> However, I think that we judge people by their professionalism, so I think a well-written note or letter will often show a very good mind and also there'll be a clarity of message when it's been well crafted, which is really important. So I think a well-thought-through memo is really important, but if it's sloppily written, in terms of not having a beginning, a middle and an end, I just think you receive it and you think what jerk wrote this?

Summary

So, we've looked in this chapter at the issue of establishing a writing personality, through raising our level of consciousness about who we are. Keep the five adjectives you've chosen near at hand to remind you about how you want to be perceived when your letter, report or e-mail is read at the far end.

Make your written words match your spoken voice wherever possible as this is most likely to preserve your credibility as people get to know you through a variety of communication channels. Honesty is important, but it is possible to be too candid!

When all else fails, be sure to rely on the principles of Plain English; if people can't understand what you're saying, they're unlikely to form a very positive opinion about you. Use the 'carpenter's rule' as a way of sense-checking what you've written and make sure at the same time that your spelling and grammar are accurate. Finally, pay attention to whom you are writing for and adapt your tone of voice to match the circumstances they'll read it in.

Try this: *Write a letter to a friend*

We have deliberately omitted advice on letter-writing from this text as so few formal letters are now sent and there are plenty of guides both on and off line which will teach you about layout. Either that, or you can rely on your word processing package to show you how.

But letter writing is a great way to practise articulating your ideas and it gives you a chance to think about grammar, punctuation, plain language and, most importantly, storytelling.

You will also be astounded by the reaction you get from your friend, as these days so few of us receive any personal letters.

The elevator test for Chapter 4

Written communication tells the reader something about you as a person, as well as the information it imparts.

Think about how you'd like others to see you – it'll guide your writing personality.

Headlines should be FACTUAL or CURIOUS – either way they must be RELEVANT to the main body of text.

An active style of writing is more engaging than a passive one – put the actor before the action.

Plain English is a critical element of written communication.

Short sentences, white space and simple phrasing produce a format that's easy to read.

Spelling and grammar are important!

Apply the carpenter's rule and check (read through) everything twice before you commit yourself (and send it).

5

Persuasion

The truth about... persuasion

How much of your communication involves persuasion? The answer, probably most of it.

You don't just find it at the sharp end of business, the sales presentation, it's happening all the time in meetings, e-mails and phone calls; we are forever trying to get other people to see things our way.

It's such a critical element that we've taken up an entire chapter talking about it and outlining how it can be done better. We've done much of this by reference to the advertising industry, where persuasion is the daily bread, and have taken our inspiration from the things that copywriters do to get our attention and then our money.

Why is advertising so important in the way we communicate? You might find this form of communication the most irritating of all, clogging up your daily paper, invading your radio listening, upsetting the continuity of your TV viewing, but advertising can teach us a huge amount about how to get our message across effectively.

According to...

Alistair Smith – Alite

> I think that advertising has got a great deal to teach communicators and public speakers in a range of different ways

because it communicates the key message creatively and through all sorts of disturbing questions, which can arise as a result of telling a story.

It can also pose a problem or engage your attention in subtle or very direct ways but it's fronting the message all the time and asking you to pay attention, so as a professional communicator it's telling you not to lose sight of the end user and to convey your message in ways that they can make sense of and transfer to their own lives.

Understanding some key principles will help you achieve the following:

■ *Cut through information overload* – your 'audience' is being fed more and more messages every day, through a seemingly endless array of new devices; how then can you make sure they take notice of what you have to say? What can you do to make them notice you?

■ *Hard-hitting key messages* – if you can find a way of stripping your communication down to its bare essentials and discover techniques that will emphasize the key issues you are more likely to be effective.

■ *The art of persuasion* – answering the question, why should people see things your way? What arguments can you put up to convince others to your point of view? How do you go about constructing that rationale?

■ *Accurately interpret the messages you receive* – knowledge of the techniques used in advertising should help you understand the communications in your inbox. You'll be better able to see the truth beyond the spin, all of which helps when you're crafting a reply.

What makes advertising work?

> Only half of advertising works, the trick is knowing which half.
>
> *Henry Ford*

From this you will gather that it's not an exact science; if it were, a lot of advertising executives would be out of work.

Experience can teach you about things like the timing of the message, the audience it's aimed at and the content of the advertisement, but there are other aspects that are much harder to pin down, like the human psyche and how the brain processes data and information.

We start by looking at what is currently known about the principles of effective advertising; once we've got an understanding of that we can think about how it applies to our own everyday communication.

The truth about... the target audience

One of the most important lessons we can learn from the world of advertising is the significance of your target audience for any piece of communication.

It is one of the fundamental rules that you must keep the reader in mind throughout the process.

According to...

Russell Grossman – BBC

> You have to remember in most organizations the audience is so diverse that there can be no single model of communication, so the way you communicate has to be adaptable.

For now though, consider how the type of person you are writing for might influence the way you put your message across. It is only when you have some empathy with the recipient that you can begin to understand how they will 'consume' what you've sent.

How would you react to the two different scenarios below?

1. Your mother is retired and sees you roughly one weekend in four as she lives some distance away – you decide you'll keep in touch more regularly by writing letters to her.
2. Your boss has to go to a meeting in an hour's time to justify this month's sales figures, which are 10% below target. She has asked you to e-mail her with the reasons you believe this has happened.

Of course the content of the two pieces of correspondence will differ hugely, but you also need to take account of the circumstances of the person reading your message.

In the first scenario the reader has time on her hands and is interested in the detail, even the trivia, of your existence.

In the second example there is an urgency that demands succinct, accurate information that can easily be interpreted and digested.

Sometimes you are trying to get a message across to a range of audiences and that is when life gets difficult. Keith Harris has extensive experience of the finance industry and became Chairman of the English Football League in August 2000.

The expert panel

Keith Harris – former Chairman of the Football League

When I worked in finance, the audience I was communicating with was broadly within a range of quite narrow parameters. However, the population of people you're communicating with in football is very diverse and the parameters very wide. Not only is the breadth huge, but within it the mix is unbelievably different and that's whether you're dealing with the public at large or the chairmen or with regulators – it's very, very tough.

It's made even more difficult because the needs of the fans aren't the same as the needs of the chairmen, and you also have to realize that the management of the clubs, both commercially and financially, is very poor.

We sought further corroboration of this by interviewing the Managing Director of Arsenal Football Club, Keith Edelman, whose background was in retailing as Chief Executive of Storehouse plc.

The expert panel

Keith Edelman – Arsenal FC

I think retailing and football are similar in that they both deal with the consumer.

The major difference is that in retailing you have to win your consumer from the competition and you have to keep on doing that – in football, you've got to manage your consumer because people don't change teams just because you put your prices up or you're not playing as well; people tend to stay with a club for life.

That leads you to communicate in a different way, it's more friendly, it's more intimate because you are literally all part of the same club in the widest sense.

I think many retail organizations would die to have the kind of relationship with their customers that we have with our fans, but I think that they'd find when they'd got it they might wonder about it.

I'll give an example: if you increase the ticket price here at Arsenal, which you could sell five times over, people will write in and say this is a ridiculous increase, why have you done it, and you explain it involves the economics of the business – they will still renew the season ticket; but the issue is that they want to get something off their chest.

If it happens in retail there's much less intimate a relationship, so if people still want it they'll buy it, but they're unlikely to complain because they know they have free choice in a retail environment to go somewhere else. In a football environment, they don't have free choice.

The truth about... making your advertisement work

In an overcrowded and competitive marketplace, three factors need to coincide to maximize your chance of being noticed above the other players:

- Reach – how many people are able to receive your message at any one time?
- Frequency – how often will people receive your message?
- Quality of message – how appealing is it?

Go back to basics and think about these factors in terms of the stallholder at the local open-air market. A big booming voice is likely to be an asset as it carries further, reaching a larger number of people.

Stand nearby for a few minutes and you'll hear the same messages repeated again and again. This has two benefits: firstly, it's a constant reminder of the key things the barker wants you to remember, and secondly, it takes account of the fact that in a bustling marketplace different people are moving in and out of earshot all the time.

Finally, consider the stallholder who is known as a local character; he/she indulges in endless amusing banter with passers-by. Even if they are slightly more expensive than the competitor at the other end of the market, you will enjoy the buying experience more.

The circus ringmaster and newspaper salesman employ the same skills, and it's only a short leap from there to many of today's commercial radio campaigns.

The truth about... creativity

If you've ever been involved in arranging advertising you will know that the media that carry commercials base their rates on the audience they deliver. Broadcast media tend to evaluate campaigns on the basis of frequency too, as the number of times the consumer sees or hears the commercial is a key influence on their ability to recall it, leading to an increase in sales of the product.

Today's audience measurement software, which is used to assess campaigns, is extremely sophisticated; it is, if you like, the *science* of advertising. The *art* comes into the last of our three elements, that of quality of message.

There seems to be no way of accurately assessing what will capture the public's imagination, no magic formula that can be applied to any product to make it stand out from the crowd. Really great advertisements, though, are likely to be one or more of the following:

■ spectacular
■ interesting
■ fashionable
■ new
■ different
■ funny.

Humour is a fantastic way of engaging an audience, but it's risky too.

Cinzano Bianco

The 1970s saw a boom in the sales of vermouth, with the Cinzano and Martini brands battling it out, head to head. A series of classic commercials was produced using popular comic actor Leonard Rossiter and classy English actress Joan Collins who was well known for character roles that were sophisticated and self-assured. Each in the series of commercials built on the last, the running gag being that Collins always ended up having the glass of Cinzano spilt down the front of her expensive dress.

In spite of the amount of attention the campaign attracted (everybody was talking about it), it resulted in increasing the sales of the competitive Martini product, for the simple reason that too much of the focus was on the humour and too little on the brand itself.

How to write great copy

There is a massive benefit in being able to write great advertising copy and you should find that the techniques we discuss below can be applied to other forms of writing too.

CASE STUDY

THE COMPANY CAR

Let's say you need to get support for a project you're working on, appeal for a greater allocation of resources, or put together a compelling argument for why you should have a company car; whatever it is, you can use the knowledge of how advertising works to add weight to the case.

Taking a brief

We start with the first step, taking the brief. In the real world of advertising this process can take a lot of time and effort but without it you have no starting point for your writing.

Brief-taking can be simplified into an a, b, c process, as you'll see below:

a Who are we talking to?
b What do we want them to do?
c Why should they do it?   *continued overleaf*

Before we examine those three simple questions in more detail, there is a golden rule that must always be applied, which is: Is 'c' a good enough reason to make 'a' do 'b'? – if not start again!

This will be easier to understand in practice, so let's apply the principles to the issue of convincing your boss that you need a company car.

The brief will be answered in the following way:

a Who are we talking to?

My immediate boss

b What do we want them to do?

Exercise his/her discretion over the company car budget and provide me with a vehicle

c Why should they do it?

■ I already claim mileage allowance when I use my car on company business at a much higher rate than the cost of running a company vehicle.

■ Each month for the last six my business mileage has increased, as I get more involved with visiting customers.

■ I am now regularly asked to represent my team at the monthly meeting in Swindon (240 miles round trip).

■ I understand that there is a shortage of my kind of skills in Swindon and I may at some point be asked to do a day or two a week there.

■ I am currently considering changing my car as it is old and unreliable, and to do this I would need to consider a finance option.

■ Last month my car broke down on the way to Swindon and I only arrived in time to catch the last five minutes of the meeting.

■ I have achieved all my objectives for the last two years and would see this as the company recognizing and rewarding my efforts.

■ On days when I am based in our main office, other members of staff could use the vehicle as a pool car.

We can't emphasize enough the application of the golden rule: Is 'c' a good enough reason to make 'a' do 'b'? – if not, start again!

If you had answered question 'c' with 'my friends will be impressed that I'm driving a brand new car' or 'Lynne got a car last month and she's only been here less than a year' you are unlikely to convince 'a' to do 'b'.

The most important thing you've done here is to present the business case to make the decision easy, ie providing a car will save the company money in the long run and make you more efficient.

You might expect your boss to put your reasons through a rigorous inspection to make sure they stand up, so you may want to provide a more in-depth financial analysis yourself.

Often decisions aren't clear-cut and you have to try to see what underlies the logic. In this case your boss will be trying to ensure that this decision is SEEN to be fair on business grounds (so that any hint of favouritism can be dispelled).

You can check your understanding of this process by taking part in the next exercise. Again, we've presented a brief with our three-stage process. This time it's up to you to write the copy (in the form of a letter) in no more than 250 words. You can then compare your version with the one we've written and make a list of the similarities and differences.

Strictly speaking, there's no right and wrong, but what you do need to look for is a well-argued case for what you propose, which covers the main reasons why your audience should do what you ask.

Exercise – writing better copy

You work for a company that manufactures nails and are just about to launch Supa-nail, a revolutionary new product made from hardened kryptonite with a smooth silicon coating that allows the nail to be knocked in quicker.

Your boss has given you the job of inviting your top 50 existing customers to a launch reception aimed at demonstrating the benefits of the new product, with the expectation that orders will follow. The invitation is to be sent out in the form of a letter.

The brief is as follows:

a Who are we talking to?
   Existing customers who use our nails in a variety of applications with the main purpose of holding things together.

b What do we want them to do?
   Attend the launch of Supa-nail so that we can show them the benefits of the new product, in the hope that they will spend more with us in future.

c Why should they do it?
   ■ There are strong personal relationships between our company and many of its customers.
   ■ This is a chance to see a revolutionary new product and to be an 'early adopter' of it, which will make you appear more dynamic to your own customers.
   ■ On the night there will be a prize draw where you can win your weight in Supa-nails.
   ■ Because of the way they are made, Supa-nails are faster to use and more reliable – lower failure rates of your end-product help to reduce costs.
   ■ You will have a chance to network with potential new partners, as well as rubbing shoulders with your competitors. (See note below.)
   ■ You will get an insight into the advantages of the new product and as such may be able to develop applications that will give you the edge in your own marketplace.

Additional background information

Your company has been facing stiff competition from abroad. Imported nails are cheaper, though there is some evidence of higher failure rates as they are made of inferior quality material (some of them are rubber).

Your customer base is loyal in the main, although some now have a mix of suppliers, including the cheaper overseas companies.

Note: It's worth putting this in the brief but you may choose to play it down in the final invitation, on the basis that it may put off as many customers as it encourages – they may feel nervous of the competition and protective of their own 'trade secrets'.

Our version of the letter is set out below, but resist the temptation to look at it until you've written your own.

Dear Mr So-and-so,

PRODUCT INNOVATION SET TO REVOLUTIONIZE OUR INDUSTRY

We'd like you to join us for the launch of Supa-nail on Wednesday 22 January so you can be one of the first to see this revolutionary new product.

For many years our industry has relied on conventional nails for fixing things together and although adequate for most needs we have become increasingly aware of the problems caused by failure rates. This has been especially true in the economy nail sector, resulting in downtime for many of our customers.

In response to this, our innovation team has developed Supa-nail, combining the toughness of kryptonite with the smooth finish of a silicon coating, for faster entry.

We'd value your attendance on the night, when you'll be able to do the following:

- See Supa-nail in action and try it for yourself.
- Discuss how Supa-nail can increase productivity in existing applications.
- Talk to the Supa-nail development team about new applications.
- Network with industry colleagues.
- Give yourself competitive advantage when you invest in Supa-nails.

In addition to all this we'll be holding a prize draw during the evening where you can WIN YOUR WEIGHT IN SUPA-NAILS!

The event will run from 18:30 to 20:00 hours at our Head Office in Slough. We look forward to seeing you then.

RSVP

Yours sincerely

Your own version of the letter will no doubt differ, but check to see if you've covered the main principles. Think about whether you've talked the language of the target audience; have you gone on to tell them what you want them to do? Most important of all, have you succinctly outlined the reasons they should do it? Does the data you've provided them with offer enough of an incentive to attend?

Look again at the letter we've written and you'll find the following practical and creative elements:

- Headline – something to draw the reader in, a summary of what this is all about.
- Empathy – created by showing understanding of some of the problems that the recipient is facing.
- Call to action – what do you want them to do?
- Summary – bullet points that give all the information quickly and succinctly.
- Reward – an incentive that answers the question 'what's in it for me?'
- Logistics – when, where.

How much puff?

It has always been accepted that there will be a degree of licence taken with advertising, showing products and services in their best light to attract the customer. The term for this is 'advertising puff'. Legal precedent in the UK was set in this area by a very famous case.

Carlill and Carbolic Smoke Ball Company – all puff and nonsense?

A good story

This important case in English law dates back to 1893.

The wonderfully named Carbolic Smoke Ball Company advertised that anyone who bought their product, used it in the directed manner and still caught influenza within a year would receive £100 (a lot of money at the time).

Mrs Carlill did just this and wrote, no doubt between her coughs and sneezes, to claim her 'compensation'. The company argued a point of law to do with offer and acceptance, claiming that no reasonable person would consider their advertisement to have been an offer capable of being accepted. In addition, they said that their advertisement had not been an offer at all, but was merely promotional 'puff'. The judges disagreed with both of these points and Mrs Carlill took her place in legal history and, no doubt, her £100 too.

The line between what is and isn't acceptable is quite thin, but a good guide is that the more specific and exaggerated the claim, the more likely it is to fall foul of the law.

How advertising has changed the way we communicate

The relevance of all this to our daily communications is that it makes us more inclined to take things with a pinch of salt; we're far more likely to ask, 'What's the catch?' In turn this makes it more and more difficult to make an impact when we're asking other people to believe our claims.

Under these circumstances it's all the more important to stick to the a, b, c rules of answering the brief, whether it's selling the case for more flexible working hours to your team or persuading your peers to share information more readily with the group.

To illustrate what we've been talking about in this chapter, here's a relevant anecdote.

The best advertisement ever written

Think about all the rules of good advertising, about how you need to target your message as specifically as possible to your particular audience, hit them with it as often as you can and have the right creative treatment to help them remember it.

The best advertisement ever written was a poster on a hoarding on a main route into Manchester in the mid-nineties.

It simply had three massive letters filling the entire space, and said

OTS

A good story

This campaign was aimed at media buyers, the people who recommend the most effective kind of advertising for their clients. One of the key methods of assessing the likely success of a campaign is to calculate the number of times your target audience is likely to see the advertisement (it's called 'frequency' and we covered it earlier), and this is usually done on historical data. In poster advertising this is referred to as OTS or 'opportunities to see', and the higher the OTS the greater the predicted success of the campaign.

What this poster said in effect was, 'Use poster advertising for your clients' business'.

It was superbly targeted, as only those in the know in advertising would understand what OTS stood for; each time they passed it they made a mental note of the opportunities to see and the very fact that they made the connection suggests that the quality of message was superb.

An example of a creative treatment that was supreme in its simplicity.

Try this: *Watch the TV commercials*

If you can't get through the second half of your favourite soap opera without a fresh cup of coffee in your hand then go out and buy a flask.

The really essential viewing for the committed communicator is TV advertising. Pro rata this is the most expensive form of television production, even outstripping costume drama on a second-for-second basis.

What that translates to is highly sophisticated messages, delivered in an alluring (and hugely expensive) way to a particular and individual group of viewers with a specific desired outcome (that they will buy the product).

Add to that list the fact that mostly the advertiser has only 30 seconds or less to get this across and you can start to appreciate the skill of the communicators involved.

Of course, it's not all high art but with such huge sums of money involved it's usually very well thought out.

While you're watching, try to work out what was in the minds of the creators: who were they aiming this advertisement at and what did they want the target group to feel after they'd seen it? Make a note of your best and worst commercials and find a mentor, friend or colleague to discuss them with.

You can add some value to this exercise by deliberately including examples that are not aimed at you. Look at how some products are aimed at the opposite sex, or take time out to watch children's TV and see what they are being asked to buy and what methods are used to convince them.

The elevator test for Chapter 5

Advertising can teach us valuable lessons about persuasion – a key element of effective communication.

As well as understanding WHO your audience is, you need to be aware of HOW they will consume your message.

Effective advertising campaigns comprise three elements – reach, frequency and quality of message.

Great commercials are memorable through being interesting, new, different or funny.

When making specific claims, don't over-exaggerate benefits; you'll only be found out.

Taking time to analyse commercial campaigns gives you insight into the art of persuasion.

6

Writing – the rules of the tools

E-mail

I don't want to discourage young people from feeling they can copy me on e-mails, but I wish people would use it a bit more responsibly.

Bill Dalton – CEO, HSBC

Most of the written communication you undertake will be in the form of e-mail; if that's not the case right now, it soon will be.

If you were working in the days before e-mail became virtually universal, you will probably remember how it was viewed as something of a curiosity. Very soon however, it became the most popular form of written communication, firstly within organizations and then in dealings with suppliers, customers and other stakeholders. One executive illustrated the speed of acceptance of this new delivery channel with the following story:

> When my son reached 4 years of age he went through a phase of asking each evening, 'What did you do at work today, Daddy?' One night I had been through the usual round of explanations, delivered in language he'd understand (I spoke to some people on the phone, met up with some of my friends at work to talk over some things etc), then realized I had no adequate explanation for what I'd spent most of the day doing.

Finally, with a flash of inspiration, I said, 'Well, Ben, you know Daddy's laptop computer that he works on at home? Well, I wrote some letters on my computer and sent them to other people's computers' – satisfied with this explanation I sat back.

After a pause, he said: 'Daddy, why didn't you just e-mail them?'

Sadly, the speed of uptake of e-mail has only been matched by the speed of abuse of it. It seems now that most people in business aren't sure whether to treat it as friend or foe. Here we set out the case for both sides.

The truth about... e-mail problems
The case for the prosecution

- *Well, if you want my opinion* – this sums up the reply-all syndrome. At its worst, this can happen when the organization wants to communicate with all staff at the same time, perhaps over a controversial issue, like cost reduction or a matter of ethics. Having had everyone's e-mail address dumped into the 'To' field, some people simply can't resist the opportunity to let the world know how they feel. So they reply-all with their 'I think this is outrageous' stance.
- *Look how hard I work* – technology has allowed an all-hours culture to develop in lots of organizations as people can log on from home at any time. If you're regularly receiving e-mail from your boss in the small hours of the morning, it won't be long before you feel duty bound to match their diligence. That said, the technology now also allows you to write an e-mail and set a time for it to be sent, so by the time your boss's request hits your inbox they could be sound asleep!
- *Stonewalling* (a defence mechanism) – considering e-mail is a virtually instantaneous method of communication, it's amazing how it can slow down any process or decision making. One trick that is often employed is deliberately to misinterpret the question being asked or to ask continually for further clarification of certain points.

- *Too shy for words* – e-mail has turned some party animals into shrinking violets as they hide behind their screen, hunched over the keyboard all day. It's not uncommon for people at adjacent desks to e-mail each other rather than engage in that age-old communication method, the conversation.
- *Spamming the boss* (for overload) – when people really don't like their boss they can use e-mail to tie them up in knots. This is especially true if there is collaboration within the team, where they agree between them that they'll all send as much e-mail (relevant or otherwise) as they can to the boss and, where possible, call for action to be taken. Even if the only action necessary is a reply, this in itself can use up massive amounts of management time.
- *I can't tell you this to your face* – cowards use e-mail to deliver the kind of bad news that should be handled sensitively and on a face-to-face basis. People have actually been made redundant on e-mail and it's all too easy to undermine individuals in this way.
- *I'm so annoyed with you* – handling conflict is an area that lots of people are really bad at. E-mail allows them to shout at colleagues, subordinates, even the boss, without ever having to face down the situation. The copying in of other parties can add to the humiliation of the intended recipient and, worse still, there's a verbatim record of what's been said that any of the parties can forward on to others as a kind of cruel voyeuristic sport.
- *Now it's your problem* – some people feel they can dump their workload on to others by e-mail (they'd call it delegation). Being at the receiving end of a list of tasks to complete at the end of a long week can be more than a little frustrating, especially when you know the other party is going home to enjoy a guilt-free weekend having cleared their inbox into yours.
- *Access all areas* (getting to the CEO) – who you could reach used to be limited by your position in the hierarchy, but no more. Now you can get to everyone whenever you want. What might seem relevant to the sender can sometimes be

of little relevance or importance to the recipient and if this results in them not replying it leaves staff with the feeling that their views aren't listened to.

According to...

Bill Dalton – HSBC

> I'm Chief Exec of HSBC Bank plc – and this bank's got 50,000 people, and before e-mail, people who work in the bowels of the organization wouldn't think of sending me a copy of their latest work, but they do now.
>
> Before, to send something on paper to me was a big deal, now it's easy, it might even be cool, but the main reason that people do that is it gives them a chance to put something in front of the Chief Exec that they never had a chance to put in front of them before.
>
> But what most people don't tell you is what really happens to all that e-mail; for example, I know other companies where the CEO has said that they welcome e-mail from everyone in the organization and that sounds wonderful, but unfortunately it's only going one way.
>
> They actually have someone in their office looking at those e-mails and saying 'hey, look at what this bozo wants', so I don't want to do that, I want to be honest with the people who work in this bank.

■ *I've got written proof* ('Well, I sent you the e-mail, look I can prove it') – of course your sent items box can be a great comfort if you've forgotten whether or not you've actioned something; equally, it can be turned to bad effect to catch other people out and the fact that all e-mails are timed and dated gives even more ammunition if your request hasn't been actioned.

According to...

Bill Dalton – HSBC

> There's an awful lot of upward delegation going on because if I don't look at a particular e-mail, if I ignore it and there's something in there that goes badly wrong six months from

now, the person that sent it to me will say, it was in the e-mail, so that's a problem.

Many of the negative aspects of e-mail were highlighted during our interviews with experts. Perhaps the most charming were the aesthetic objections from one source.

According to...
Keith Harris – Seymour Pierce/Football League

> I'm not a big fan of e-mail. I've always been averse to screens. I've got a beautiful antique desk and I don't want some poxy screen on it.

Finally, a few experts expressed the following opinion but didn't want it attributed to them!

> I wish there was a button you could press which sent an automatic reply saying, you're confusing me with someone who gives a damn!
>
> *Anon*

The truth about... e-mail benefits
The case for the defence

■ *Faster than a speeding bullet* – the trouble with the conventional postal service is that everything takes so long. Now message sending and receiving is virtually instantaneous. You can be talking to someone on the phone, send them the relevant attachment, and hear the 'ping' of their inbox as it arrives.

■ *Let's be friends* – because of the way e-mail has evolved it tends to be much less formal than other kinds of written communication and as a consequence much friendlier. Used well, it can be a great way of engaging people very quickly.

■ *More than words can say* – greater bandwidth is becoming more and more common, which means that e-mails are no longer restricted to the written word. Increasing amounts of data can be fed down the line, including pictures, video, graphics, presentations and more.

- *When memory loss is a problem* – 'did I call that meeting for 10 or 10:30?' With e-mail you can always check your written record, not only of what you've said to 'them', but what 'they' have asked of you.
- *Fully flexible* – now that home working has become commonplace you're not tied to the office to finish everything off. You can go home and log on, using e-mail as the primary vehicle for receiving requests from others and actioning the tasks you have to complete.
- *Hear ye! Hear ye!* – as a form of mass communication e-mail is hard to beat. It happens in real time and more importantly it's simultaneous in its delivery. This means that if you have to tell people the same story at the same time you can deliver the message to everyone's inbox in a single hit.

According to...

Michael Broadbent – Director of Group Corporate Affairs, HSBC Holdings plc

> HSBC now employs over 215,000 people worldwide, so e-mail gives you an enormous advantage over the historic tyranny of size and distance, especially when spread over 80 countries and territories.

If you're confused about whether e-mail is a good or bad thing then don't be. Of course it can be both, it's really about how well it's used that matters. Here's a balanced view from Surinder Hundal, Internal Communications Director of Nokia.

The expert panel

Surinder Hundal – Nokia

E-mail makes it much easier to communicate across time zones and across borders, so it removes some of the artificial barriers; it's also very cheap and you can do things very, very quickly. On the negative side, there is a tendency to overuse e-mail and not only in terms of the quantity of messages but also, I would argue, in the quality of messages you generate.

By that, I mean people tend to become too dependent on conducting their business through e-mail, when it may be better to think about the situation and decide if it could be handled face to face or by a phone call – I think we're also beginning to lose that skill of fitting the situation to the medium.

There can be a tendency for people to hide behind their laptops and build relationships with their computers rather than other people – especially if you're not part of a big team. We think that if you're not careful this could start to have an impact on culture, not only in terms of social culture but also in the way we actually solve problems and deal with situations.

The second aspect is one where because you're hiding behind a PC, it's easier to send an angry e-mail – it's called 'flaming'– and that's something that can get compounded and create a culture that is very direct. On e-mail you don't have any niceties like a conversation about the weather or some other social preamble.

The third aspect is that people use e-mail badly and so you get a message which has got about 400 pages of previous e-mails attached, all of which just clogs up your system.

To try to get over this at Nokia we have a basic policy of 'netiquette' that lays out some obvious 'dos' and 'don'ts', and periodically we have a burst of noise that reminds people about what is good practice.

From your own point of view you need to be aware of the good and bad of e-mail, and try to make sure that your outgoing messages don't compound the problems associated with it.

If you work as part of a small team you can also try to convert your colleagues to this way of thinking, which should go some way to improving the number and relevance of the messages hitting your inbox.

Beyond this, the 'burst of noise', referred to by Surinder Hundal, is a good way of reminding a larger group of people about the dos and don'ts of e-mail.

Try this: *Learn to touch type*

Like paying into a pension scheme or brushing your teeth, touch-typing is something you should start doing as young as you possibly can.

There are two main benefits of being able to type using all your fingers, without having to glance at the keys. The first is speed and the second is the ability to read a handwritten document, like some meeting notes you may have made, and type them up simultaneously, without having to glance backwards and forwards at the keyboard.

You can probably find lots of reasons why not to bother; for a start it's hard (especially at first), time consuming, and voice recognition is probably just around the corner... maybe.

On the other hand, it's not inconceivable that you could double your current typing speed, saving you valuable minutes or even hours each day, which could add up to months or years over the course of your lifetime.

There are lots of software packages and instruction books available and by setting aside maybe 15 minutes a day, first or last thing or during your lunch break, you'll soon get the hang of it.

One further tip: you don't even have to be that good, unless you aspire to be PA to the Managing Director. Spell and grammar checking will pick up most of your errors and you should always re-read your material before you send it out, to see if there's a better way of saying what you've said.

The last word on e-mail comes from Chris Major, Head of PR at AstraZeneca, one of the world's top five pharmaceutical companies, who sounds a warning to all of us who rely so heavily on e-mail for our business dealings and to share gossip with friends:

> I think that people sometimes naively believe that an e-mail is somehow not a public communication.

A sobering thought.

The truth about… texting

My heart misses about 300 beats per month – one for every text alert I get.

Anon

New technology is never 'new' for very long, but fortunately when it comes to communication, the rules that apply to existing methods can generally be applied to whatever comes along.

The popularity of texting took even mobile phone manufacturers Nokia by surprise and the uptake has been a modern communications phenomenon.

Early adopters of the technology were teenagers, who found that this highly intimate and secretive way of keeping in touch not only proved cheaper than standard cellphone calls but had its own mystique and even developed its own language.

The laborious process of entering each individual letter soon became obsolete as 'predictive' texting was introduced and mobile phones that could 'learn' new vocabulary were developed.

As the process became easier, so the popularity grew, and soon no first date was complete without a final flirtatious text exchange on the way home.

Some commercial organizations were quick to seize on this new way of reaching customers and less scrupulous users started to find ways of exploiting the medium, either by getting unsuspecting recipients to reply to premium rate numbers or by a whole pile of other money-grabbing schemes.

The following pages look at texting as a way of communicating and examine the pros and cons of the technology.

We start by describing the growth of the mobile phone and current attitudes towards it. Early examples of this technology could only just be called 'mobile' as the batteries were so large (and external to the phone itself) that you needed an intensive course at the gymnasium just to be able to carry them. No doubt phone theft was much less then, as the average mugger wouldn't have the strength to run away with it.

We now find ourselves at the other end of the spectrum, with some people complaining that the keys have become too small to operate and a vast number of phones lost every year, simply because they are so tiny – certainly countless of them have been placed on the roof of the car and the driver sped off forgetting where they left it.

The truth about... criteria for texting

When you're thinking about the 'who', 'what', 'where' and 'why' of texting, the most important factor to remember is how intensely personal a device the mobile phone is. Before mobiles were invented, the house or office phone was accepted as a shared piece of equipment used for communication. Now people are far more likely to see their mobile as their individual access to others on a one-to-one basis.

This attitude is likely to harden as phones become more sophisticated. They already carry 'my ring tone', 'my graphics', 'my address book' and as picture and videophones become more commonplace they are increasingly becoming a record of who we are and how we live our lives.

The intimate nature of texting between friends adds further to the protective feelings people have for their phone, so you have to be very sure of your ground before sending any unsolicited messages.

According to...

Surinder Hundal – Nokia

> In Finland, mobile phone ownership is almost 100% and people do develop a sort of relationship with their mobile. I talk to teenage children in Finland and they say they feel naked without their phone; they would rather lose their set of the house keys than their phone. They said when they leave the house the first thing they pick up is their phone, then their wallet or purse and keys.

There are signs that some trust is starting to build between organizations who have an existing relationship with their customers, so more and more we see banks offering text services to update balances or warn of an impending descent into the red. However, in nearly all cases these services are employed on a 'by invitation only' basis, in that customers actively have to register with the bank in order to receive the updates.

Even providing information can have its pitfalls. A chain of estate agents started texting potential purchasers with details of houses that might suit their needs. Although the recipients understood why the service was being provided, they had not given express permission ('by invitation only') to the estate agent, and the problem was made worse once a suitable property had been found (often via another agent) yet the messages continued to come through.

One recipient put how he felt into words like this:

> I knew they were only trying to help and part of me thought it was okay as I had willingly given them my mobile number, but I honestly thought they'd just use it for arranging viewings.
>
> We'd been house-hunting for some time and every time my text-beep went off I thought it might be my girlfriend to say she'd found something suitable – that just doubled my disappointment when I discovered that it was another poor match from the estate agent – it felt like being spammed on your phone.
>
> In the end we found our house through another agent.

We also need to understand the 'physical limitations' of texting if we are to get the most from it. There is a finite size of text message bound by the number of characters that may be entered. In reality, because of small screen sizes and the need to scroll it's probably dangerous to fill the outgoing message to capacity – by the time the recipient has read to the end they may have forgotten the beginning!

At its best a text message should be some kind of alert, like an invitation, an apology or to show empathy. Before you decide to send a business text, think about the benefits:

- Texting is very personal – people will know that you're their friend.
- Texting is quick – great as a follow-up to more formal communication.

- Texting is succinct – it gets simple messages across effectively.
- Texting is incisive – it cuts through the 'noise' of other communications.

Here are some examples of good use of text in business situations:

- To say 'well done' to a member of your team.
- To announce a result – 'we won the sales pitch!'
- To empathize with a colleague – 'sorry the boss gave you a bad time!'
- To impart information – 'yes, Friday at noon is fine by me!'

We don't recommend using text to say 'you're sacked!'

(NB: Shortly after we wrote this, the first well-publicized mass sacking, in the UK, by text message took place, as the compensation claims specialist The Accident Group made sweeping redundancies, informing their staff via their mobile phones.)

According to...

Surinder Hundal – Nokia

> Because texting someone is more remote than a face-to-face meeting, managers may feel it's an easier way of delivering bad news – you don't have to look into the 'whites of their eyes', so you feel you can get away with delivering the bad news without having to think what the repercussions would be.

So, there's good news and bad news if you're thinking of using text as a business tool. Without doubt it's set to become more and more popular, but heed the warnings above before you launch headlong into arranging all your meetings on it, or announcing a 10% discount day to all your customers.

Finally, we turn again to someone who should know a thing or two about this technology, Surinder Hundal of Nokia.

The expert panel

Surinder Hundal – Nokia

We are continually having conversations within Nokia about the social impact of what we do but sometimes you can't be sure what that'll be in advance. Take texting, for example; when we developed the Short Messaging Service, we thought it would mainly be used for business applications, like maybe checking people's availability if you were setting up a meeting – and now you get something like 8 billion text messages a month globally.

What's interesting is that quite a lot of the traffic is in messages that aren't substantive – it's almost like the equivalent of speech, people are conversing with each other through text and that is obviously a change in social behaviour.

Within Nokia we've found text really useful, particularly as an alert, so you might want to alert people to results being announced or signposting some news that might be appearing on e-mail or the intranet, so it's really a broadcast method.

The truth about... writing for the Internet

You might not have to write Web copy but this topic will help you for two reasons. First, by understanding what is good and bad, you will be better able to judge how much another organization knows or cares about its Web presence. Apart from this, the disciplines of writing good Web copy can teach us a lot about how to present other forms of written work to get the maximum attention and response from our audience.

Why the Internet is different

Our increasing usage of the Internet has led us to discover a number of key differences in the way it is consumed:

■ *It's so slow* – reading speeds are significantly diminished from a computer screen, some say by up to 30%. A number of theories have been put forward why this is. Certainly it's partly down to the 'quality' of the type; a good printer turning out high-resolution hard copy will provide you with documents that are much easier to read, but Web design has an influence too – often there's a lot of distracting clutter on a Web page that draws our eye away from the text and makes it difficult to concentrate.

■ *And it gets slower* – there are a couple of other simple but practical reasons for us slowing down: firstly, many sites are still too complex in their structure, so take a long time to download, and many use long passages of text that need to be scrolled through. Turning a page is much quicker.

■ *Usage* – think about what you use the Internet for. Is it for research, monitoring competitors, information, fun, leisure, online booking or banking, news and weather? The list goes on. In all these cases a degree of 'surfing' will probably be necessary, meaning we'll skip lightly from one page to another, from one site to the next, taking little time to stop and read anything in detail. That makes the demands of the writing style all the more rigorous.

■ *Mindset* – there's a world of difference between setting some time aside to read a 100-page report that's landed on your desk and the way that we hop in and out of cyber-space. How many times have you used the phrase, 'I'll just have a quick look on the Internet'? Now you can see the difference in how your concentration level will be for each task. Under those circumstances you have to be able to hit visitors to your own site hard and fast, give them what they want in the shortest time possible and allow them to move on.

■ *Competitive time pressure* – given the information overload (which we discuss elsewhere), we often have to resort to reading just an executive summary of everything we see. This has resulted in something of a sound-bite culture, but its increasing inevitability means that Web pages need to keep pace. Because the Internet is so vast and there are so many competing sites for every type of need, we no longer have to stick with something to see if it delivers what we're looking for. If a page downloads too slowly, has poor navigation, looks untidy or fails within milliseconds to offer us the information we're looking for, then we're off searching elsewhere.

Learn how to overcome all of this and you will have become an expert in tight, informative, entertaining writing. The techniques are simple:

■ *Upside down* – the experts say you should write Web copy in an 'inverted pyramid style', with the most important information at the top and the detail further down. This is also true of newspaper stories and advertisements – so the starting point is to get the essence of the story or offer or information across as quickly as possible; if you like, it's a kind of headline. Based on this, people will make an instant decision whether to read on or go elsewhere so you'd better get it right.

■ *Scan-tastic!* – there's lots of evidence to suggest that people don't sit and read every word of Web copy, but simply scan across it to get the essence of what is being said. You can make this much easier for them if you think about layout and try to use as much white space as possible; it really does make for easier reading.

■ *Sum it up* – bullet points are a great way of summarizing what you're saying. You could start with a couple of opening paragraphs and then go on to summarize in bullet form the core of the story or the benefit of what you're offering.

■ *No ramblers here!* – long sentences that seem to go nowhere are out. What you need are lots of short sentences that say what needs to be said. For some reason this style is much easier to read. The extra benefit is that people will remember more of what you've said.

When you've finished writing your Web copy, is it all of these things?

■ Understandable – at a glance.
■ Concise – half as many words as for any other medium.
■ Simple – Plain English.
■ Relevant – to what you'd promised.

The truth about... bullet points

Loaded with bullets – bullet point lists are commonplace, but often poorly constructed. Here are some hints on how to make your bullets better.

Firstly, remember that the list should be centred around a single theme, so it might be a collection of reasons to support an argument, or it could be something as simple as a list of names or statements.

If you were describing the virtues of a new product you could use nouns, like reliability and convenience, verbs such as enduring, or adjectives like consistent or convenient, but make sure you don't mix them or, worse still, use all three.

For design reasons your bullets should be roughly the same length; this also makes them easier to digest. It doesn't matter if you use upper or lower case, or end with a full stop or not, as long as you're consistent.

Bullet points should be used when you have a list of items all of which carry equal weight or importance.

If your text relies on a logical sequence, like instructions or directions, you should use a numbered list rather than bullet points, indicating that the points need to be followed in order.

You can adopt or adapt many of these Web writing tips and use them across the spectrum of your written communication; you'll certainly find that what you're producing is more concise and you can find out if other people like your new style by asking some of your peers for feedback.

The elevator test for Chapter 6

E-mail is fast becoming the most common form of written communication, so treat it with respect.

Make sure the e-mail you send is RELEVANT to the audience – keep it short and to the point.

Don't get drawn into a war of words on e-mail – if there's a conflict situation, sort it out face to face.

Of all new technologies, text messaging is the most personal and intimate.

Texting is good as an alert mechanism, but generally poor for communicating with customers.

Writing for the Internet requires discipline and, at most, only half the words of other written communications.

Users tend only to scan Web pages, so messages need to be punchy and design is best kept simple.

7

Listening

The truth about... listening and talking

Now we've examined the elements of the written word, it's time to move on and look at something we do instinctively and naturally, every day of our lives: listening and talking. As with the other aspects of communication that we've discussed, we aim to take this subject and move it into a more conscious state, so that you can analyse and improve on the way you do it now.

We'll then look at how to apply what we've learnt to increase the effectiveness of what we say and the usefulness of what we hear. Included in this will be sections on how to conduct phone conversations, what to look out for in meetings and ways of presenting to small or large audiences that will get your message across in a more persuasive way.

The truth about... how to listen

If you listen to everything that you hear, not just the words, but what's going on around them, you get a much richer picture.

Simon Armson – Chief Executive, Samaritans

Why don't we listen more?

According to...

John Akers – a Relate Counsellor

Most of us are not brought up to be very good listeners.

In your childhood you often come away with a sense of criticism; you come through school, there's lots of criticism, in your job there's lots of criticism and I think a lot of people become very defensive unless they're very sure of themselves.

You have to find a way of allowing people to be vulnerable without it being fatal, so that people have the opportunity to grow up and change.

General rules of listening

We deal with listening before talking for a very good reason and that's because the former informs the latter; in other words, what we say is usually governed by what has gone before, so understanding the other party's point of view helps us respond appropriately.

In addition, appearing to listen properly has the dual benefit of making the other person feel valued, while giving you enough time to formulate a suitable response. Just think how useful this technique will be in a formal interview situation.

Although there are techniques that can make you appear more attentive than you really are (which we'll outline a little later), in general terms it's hard to fake interest when there is none and even tougher to sustain that over any period of time, as the following short story illustrates.

Vital organs only

The monthly management meeting always dragged on longer than it should and the low spot was a presentation of the sales figures by Roger, the Head of Finance. The rest of the attendees tried their very hardest to look interested, but with his dull monotone, meticulous detail and lack of humour it was a trial.

After one such meeting the Head of Operations approached the Marketing Director and said, 'I saw you this afternoon during Roger's presentation; you were operating on vital organs only.'

A good story

Maybe you can relate to that feeling.

If you are faced with a similar situation, in a regularly scheduled meeting, try to manage the situation rather than waste the time. If you have sufficient influence (ie if you are the line manager of the culprit), then think about some suitable coaching, either from yourself or a third party.

If your influence is more limited then look at ways of changing behaviours. You could lead by example, producing a sparkling and interesting report when it's your turn, or ask interested questions to the other party to break the monotony.

Phrasing can be important here too; don't belittle their area of responsibility, but find an appropriate way of eliciting the information you need. Here's an example:

> 'Roger, could you just give us the overall group figures and the reasons why they appear to be down – you can e-mail the individual area numbers to us later, to digest in our own time.'

Now think up some of your own to apply to situations you might face.

Natural interest

When we truly are interested in what someone has to say we send out lots of non-verbal signals in an unconscious way. It follows, therefore, that if you consciously mimic those actions when someone is talking, they will naturally think that you are enchanted with what they are saying. Journalists, salesmen and suitors are all great at faking this behaviour, but you have already been warned: it's difficult if not impossible to keep it up for long periods.

These natural behaviours of attentiveness look like the following:

■ Make eye contact.
■ Lean forward.
■ Mirror the speaker's actions and mannerisms.
■ Keep your pose 'open'.
■ Signal frequent agreement (by nodding and smiling).

Eye contact is vitally important in making the other party aware of how interested you are; it's key in the mating game and just as important in business. We tend to judge people who won't meet our gaze as shifty and untrustworthy, but also be aware that using too much eye contact can be threatening in some situations.

Another important element of body language involves leaning in towards the speaker, as if attempting to ensure that you don't miss a single syllable of what they are saying. Be careful to make sure that all the signals are matching up; for example, someone leaning in, with an aggressive facial expression, can be threatening rather than welcoming.

Mirroring is the curious ritual we engage in which involves copying the other party in everything they do. It shows empathy in an unconscious way and signals our approval of them as an individual and of their actions.

Crossed legs or arms or a 'bunched' pose shows you are on the defensive, maybe even intimidated or afraid. Learn to relax and keep your arms and legs loose, rather than wound around each other.

If you ever watch a radio or television interview being conducted, you will see the journalist frantically and frequently nodding their agreement to keep their guest talking – they may even occasionally verbalize this with a grunt or an 'I see' or a 'how interesting' type of phrase.

If all else fails, they will often fall silent in a war of nerves. Most of us instinctively feel uncomfortable in certain social situations if silence falls; this can be a great vehicle for getting the other party to keep talking and fill the gap.

When we're genuinely animated about what someone else is saying, we show our approval by smiling – coupled with the nodding technique above, this is an irresistible signal to most speakers to keep them feeling that they are delivering awe-inspiring thoughts.

There are lots of situations where using this behaviour is helpful, including job interviews, sales pitches and meetings. There's nothing fake or phoney either, it's simply about understanding how to get the other party to open up.

In some extreme situations, the ability to listen can even be a matter of life and death. That's the case for the charity Samaritans.

The expert panel

Simon Armson – Samaritans

Any communication is a three-part process, there's a *transmission*, then there's the *medium* through which the message is transmitted and finally, there's the *reception*.

As far as Samaritans' communication is concerned, what is absolutely paramount is the ability to listen and to hear – and to be able to hear not only what's said on the lines, as it were, but also what's said between the lines.

A lot of work is done on the telephone and it surprises many people the amount of non-verbal communication that takes place on the telephone. One has to be very attuned to that, so one's hearing and listening skills have to be very carefully honed.

I think listening and hearing are two different things. You can listen by actually hearing; I don't mean just reacting to the sound waves that enter your ear, but actually hearing what's meant, what's expressed, what's not said, what the emotions are, what the feelings are that are contained within the words which you are actually listening to.

When you're on the telephone it's not just the sounds that you hear, it's the silences too, it's the noises that you hear, that aren't words, but are maybe to do with breathing, maybe to do with crying, it may be to do with sighing, it may be to do with the external environment, so you can detect where someone is, are they on the street, are they in a call box, are they in their home? Have they got the radio and television on? Is there a pet in the vicinity? Those sorts of things help you build a picture.

So I think there's an important distinction between the act of listening, which is a sort of passive act, it happens because you've got ears that work, whereas hearing is something which I believe you have to work at.

The truth about... when to listen

Shut up! – for every minute that you talk, spend two listening.

Professor David Clutterbuck

It wouldn't be natural if we tried to listen with this high degree of attentiveness all the time, nor would it be appropriate in all circumstances. When, for example, was the last time you listened to a commercial radio station with all your attention – why would you?

At the other end of the spectrum, if you were to stop and ask directions in an unfamiliar town you'd be pretty sure to concentrate on the answer.

Most business situations fit in between these two extremes; the trick is to decide where. Clearly the amount of attention you should give to any situation should be directly related to its importance. You can make your own list of criteria based on your job description and department, then add that to the four situations below:

■ first meeting
■ negotiation
■ announcements
■ hierarchical.

These require a bit of explanation. A first meeting, with a new client or supplier, or even with other departments in your own organization is critical in establishing the balance of power, so you must pay attention. Beyond that, any circumstance when negotiation is going to take place is an important one from a listening point of view, because once again you can constantly be assessing the changes in the balance of power.

Announcements will need careful attention as you may be part of the cascade process and need to interpret what is being said so you can outline the implications to peers or your own team. 'Hierarchical listening' is as simple as making sure you pay attention when the boss is speaking!

Of course, you shouldn't devote your attention solely to these situations; this is not permission to switch off when anybody else is talking. What we are saying is that there are some situations that demand your special attention.

To be really effective at this, it's a good idea to mark your diary up each day with the critical meetings when you simply must pay attention to what is happening. Try to anticipate the likely outcomes of meetings and think through the reasons they might have been called in the first place.

Under circumstances where you have control over the timing of these junctions of communication, it makes sense to arrange them in the morning, as that is the time of day when we are likely to be more attentive. If you think back to your school days the afternoon activities were often planned to be less mentally taxing (sports, art, crafts etc).

Certainly the mark of successful communicators is their ability to take a step back from a situation and listen to what's being said.

According to...

Simon Terrington – Human Capital

How much you listen and how you listen, then how much you talk and how you talk are just a fascinating balance. Confident and successful people tend to listen.

I'll give you an example: a kid is struggling at school and the kid will say, 'Dad, I hate school' and the dad will straightaway go into autobiography: 'When I was a lad, I worked hard, I was top of my class at maths, went on to get top grades in my exams...' and the kid just looks on in desperation.

And what the dad needs to say is, 'You're having a bad time at school?' and the kid can say, 'Yeah, I just don't know what I'm doing in science' or 'I can't understand the teacher', and if you have a chat about it and find out what's going on you can actually diagnose the problem and start prescribing a solution. But the idea that you'd walk into the doctor's and he'd say 'Here you go, these drugs will get you better, goodbye!' before you've even said what's wrong is ludicrous.

The elevator test for Chapter 7

Listening is more important than speaking.

Hear what others have to say first – it'll help you formulate a better response.

Learn the techniques of being attentive – apply them in appropriate circumstances.

Shut up and listen! – for every minute that you talk, spend two listening.

Decide what the critical attention moments of your working day are.

Try to keep high-attention junctions to the morning.

8

Talking

The truth about... talking

The ability to talk rather than write is very important because you can obviously communicate (ie 'share') a message far more power-fully using voice rather than text. The inflection in your voice alone reveals how you're feeling.

Russell Grossman – BBC

In this chapter we're going to examine the message and the delivery method, so we'll start with 'what you say'. Whatever your message is, try to get into the habit of chunking it into three components.

The theory of lists of three has been examined many times. Politicians and orators use it over and over again when speaking, keeping their message within the confines of a three-point plan.

There are two ways of looking at this (though it would fit better if there were three!). We all know that attention spans are limited, and it seems that the more information overload we face, the worse it gets. Even 'hard news' programmes are forced into cutting items down to bite-sized pieces for us to consume.

The second issue is this. If you were to say to someone that you had just one thing to tell them, that thing would be regarded as very important indeed. If you were·to say that you had 10 messages to put across then each would be a tenth as important as if it were a single message. So, the more separate messages you try to communicate, the less importance will be attributed to each individual point – it's just not worth risking more than three.

If this seems inconvenient because you have just finished drawing up your 12-point plan for success, then you should think about how you could present it as being a three-stage plan, each of which has a number of sub-sections (four in each in fact).

When you sit down to formulate your message you need to put yourself in the position of the listener; how will your communication be decoded and consumed? What you say will be governed by many factors, some of which are listed below – you will be able to add your own according to the type of organization you work for:

■ How much do you know?
■ Who else needs to know?
■ How much do you need to tell them?
■ Is there any reason to be secretive?
■ What will be the impact? (on morale? on the way we operate?)
■ Is there any commercial sensitivity?
■ How important is timing?
■ What is the balance of risk? (saying nothing can sometimes be dangerous)

Learn from the people around you, including your boss, your peers, your staff. Only you can decide where to draw the lines, but think about where honesty oversteps the mark into indiscretion. At what point does genuine concern for others lapse into a desire to gossip about their private life? What impact does an unhealthy secrecy have on other people?

The truth about... how you say it

I think it's a good idea to come up with a single sentence on any project you're involved with – it's a great way of making sure you're able to deliver the message very quickly and it has the added benefit that it focuses your own mind.

Professor Cary Cooper

Once you have decided on what the message is, how do you put it across? You need to consider both the form of words you choose and the physical elements of delivery. The starting point is to distil the message down to its bare essentials, in much the same way as we've done in the summaries at the end of chapters, entitled the elevator test.

This tends to focus your attention on what is really important – it's a great way of honing your messages into their core elements.

Some of the most effective communicators decide on their message in advance of any communication and then deliver it relentlessly. Senior managers at Microsoft undergo media training, and you can tell. Irrespective of the issue that's being discussed, they will tell you how that relates to the way things are done in Microsoft; they even use the company name with great frequency.

Listen to politicians being interviewed and it's rare for them to answer the question with anything other than the message they want to get across. This is how it's done.

According to...

Derek Hatton – broadcaster and ex-politician

> If you're being interviewed for tonight's news and you know that there's one single point you want to make and someone comes out to interview you and the point you want to put across is – the shirt I am going to wear is black, then it goes like this...
>
> 'But Mr Hatton, why was it that when you did that, there was an immediate drop in the share price?'
> 'The shirt that I'm going to wear is black.'
> 'But Mr Hatton, why is it that Everton didn't get into Europe?'
> 'The shirt that I'm going to wear is black.'
> When that reporter gets back to the studio and his editor says 'What have you got?', he'll say 'I've got "the shirt he wants to wear is black".' 'What?!' says the editor, 'Well, if that's all you've got then, oh f***, I'll have to use it.'

It may be that under many mundane circumstances you just need to get on with delivering what you have to say in the most succinct and matter of fact way; there may be little room for window-dressing.

However, some types of message may need more impact and then it's worth considering a more theatrical approach. Sometimes this is also dependent on the surroundings and nature of the presentation.

In a one-to-one or small meeting, this kind of melodrama would be inappropriate, but if you were faced with engaging with a large audience and keeping them interested for an extended period of time (particularly if you are speaking directly after a large lunch) you might need to consider some of the following dramatic techniques:

▪ comedy
▪ drama
▪ suspense
▪ mystery
▪ action
▪ thrills.

If you want to learn more about these techniques then raise your level of consciousness when you watch a movie or a live theatre show and ask yourself what it is about the action that inspires particular feelings within you – why do you feel scared, tense, happy, moved? What is happening within the performance to spark these emotions? A greater understanding will help you emulate these techniques in your own 'performance'.

As with all forms of communication, take heed of the type of audience you are addressing and consider their level of familiarity with the topic, the mix of gender, their average age and the level they've reached within the organization – try hard to imagine what it's like for them receiving the message and you'll get a much better feel for whether you've pitched it right.

The truth about... rehearsed and unrehearsed speech

Don't get too concerned with thinking that you can never again open your mouth to speak without first having run the up-and-coming sentence through a rigorous vetting process. We indulge in unrehearsed speech all the time and a good thing too. It is our instinctive reaction to what is going on around us. We use it for much of our day-to-day business, we give our opinions, pass on knowledge and respond to the ever-changing situations we encounter. The only thing we would urge when it comes to this type of communication is that once in a while you stop and think about how you sound.

Are there times when you are too flippant, sarcastic, pompous, serious, demanding or even plain boring? It's hard to assess these kinds of behaviours in ourselves but unforgivable that we should not occasionally try. Being aware of how you sound and sensitive to how your audience may interpret your messages goes a long way towards making you a great communicator.

At the other extreme, there is the meticulously planned and well-rehearsed presentation. You may have repeated this to yourself many times, even in front of the mirror or a trusted colleague, and will have had an opportunity to apply a more rigorous and objective set of criteria to what you're saying and the way you're saying it. But in between there are many more occasions when you can raise your level of consciousness and 'rehearse' what you are going to say.

A quiet five minutes before the start of a meeting to review your notes and visualize how you will deliver them will go a long way to making you more articulate and sure of your ground.

The elevator test for Chapter 8

Because the voice can convey so much it's easier to persuade through talking than writing.

Sticking to lists of three helps audiences grasp your message more easily.

Think hard about your target audience, what they'll need or want to know, how they'll respond to what you say.

Distil your core message down to its shortest form – think about what it is you're really saying.

Theatrical techniques can bring your speech to life – make sure the context is appropriate.

Occasionally try to hear yourself as other people hear you and analyse how you sound.

9

Listening and talking – the rules of the tools

Sometimes we listen, sometimes we talk, mostly we do both.

Now we're going to examine the difference between face-to-face communication and occasions when you can't see the other party, like during a telephone conversation.

What's the difference? Communication is a two-way process and in order to be more effective at sending 'messages' to the other party, we need to be sensitive to how they are receiving them. What people say out loud does not always tie up with how they feel inside.

The marriage guidance service Relate has a mass of experience of people failing in their communication. You ask your partner, 'how are you?' and get the answer, 'fine!' but is it borne out in their body language? The chances are you know right away if things aren't okay. The mismatch between verbal and non-verbal messages stands out a mile.

Tone of voice, posture, facial expression, lack of eye contact can all be signs that things are far from 'fine'.

Each of us has our own threshold in dealing appropriately with this, according to the relationship we are in. There are times when it is worth pursuing the enquiry to discover what the matter really is, and times when it is not. The book stores are packed with volumes that deal with this topic, but it's far too risky territory for us!

Failing to address the issues can lead to a spiral of non-communication to the point where the two people involved can no longer relate to each other at all. The specialist help of marriage guidance is often called upon just to get the parties talking again, to teach them how to communicate.

According to...

John Akers – a Relate Counsellor

> Listening and talking are very important because I would say that largely speaking, poor communication is one of the main reasons why relationships break down.

When we can see people reacting to what we are saying we have more clues to how they are actually feeling and can adapt as we go, in order to get the outcome we want.

The telephone doesn't allow us to do that, but in certain circumstances people can become attuned to the mood of the other party, simply by experience of listening and talking to many people on the phone.

We saw this earlier in the quote from Simon Armson of Samaritans, but in less dire circumstances the same skills can still be applied.

This happens most obviously in the best of call centres, like for example banking pioneers First Direct.

Technology + personality = success

Telephone banking has been made possible by computer technology which delivers the kind of information the operator needs about the caller's account, in a usable format and at great speed.

When it comes to the ideal people for the job, First Direct take an approach whereby they recruit for attitude and train for skill. This means they get the right kind of people in the first place, and then equip them with the tools and training to do the job.

This results in scenarios like the following one.

The marriage proposal

A caller had conducted a number of routine transactions like paying bills and checking balances, and was pleased to hear that his redundancy cheque had cleared, leaving him with some financial security. He thought the call was over, when this happened:

Operator: Just before you go, Mr May, can I ask you a question?

Caller: (expecting it to be some advice about how to invest the money) Yes, of course.

Operator: I see from your account that a large sum has just been paid in and I was wondering…

Caller: Yes?

Operator: Will you marry me?!

The point of the story is that having the confidence to joke around with customers is born out of the experience of being able to read them, in a particular situation. In this case, it was a mixture of evidence provided by the technology of the large balance, added to an assessment of the type of person the caller was (picked up during the early routine transactions) that made the operator take the risk of the joke – she later confessed to the caller that she was happily married with five children!

For most of us, we take the telephone for granted, but we're not yet attuned to it with the effectiveness of a good call centre operator. How do we use the phone better and communicate more effectively with it?

The telephone used to be a fixed piece of equipment, and calls were regarded as an event, but now no one is self-conscious about walking down the street chatting to friends or conducting business and it is precisely because of this that we have become complacent about the power of the telephone. Also, there is now an expectation that we are always available, so it would be hard to classify any telephone conversation as an event, it's just part of our daily lives.

However, we need to recognize that there are a number of significant differences between inbound and outbound calls:

- You have little or no control over inbound calls – they can come at any time.
- You have no idea what to expect when you pick up the phone.
- With inbound calls the other party has set the agenda for discussion.
- Inbound calls are often disruptive to good time management.

Because of these differences, you need to make provision in your working day to handle the situation. Again, technology looked like it had provided a solution, at least for a while. Now, however, we regard voicemail and voice-activated menus as the scourge of our age; most of us just want to talk to a real person again! There's advice on how to get the best from voicemail later in this chapter.

In some organizations managers have been known to be in their office the whole day and rather than answer the phone and be interrupted, have left voicemail on the whole time, checking in now and again to see if anyone interesting enough to warrant a call back has phoned.

It is much better to learn how to handle human beings who call than to ignore them, and because you can never be sure what to expect when you pick up a ringing phone, you have to be prepared to cope with uncertainty.

The truth about... inbound calls

Here are some techniques for managing incoming calls as a necessary (in fact vital) part of your working day.

Ask yourself who is calling. How important are they? How much of your time do they usually take up? Are they concise and efficient in their dealings or are they the office gossip?

How much time do you have? Sometimes it's good to take time to chat on the phone; you can find out a lot of important information this way. If, on the other hand, you've got a busy day you need to have your own stock phrases for cutting the conversation short.

Make an early assessment of the point of the call. Once you've done this, you're far more likely to be in control, by offering some options on how the enquiry can best be resolved.

With regular callers who have routine enquires that are important without being urgent you can ask that they always call you at a particular time ('You'll find it's easier to get me after about 4 pm. My meetings have usually finished by then') or even ask them to e-mail you as you can then fit their enquiry into a time-managed e-mail block.

Another strategy is to arrange call sharing with a close colleague and agree to answer the phones on an hour-by-hour basis. In this way, you can do some 'call filtering', eg 'if the boss rings then put them through, if it's Nicholas in accounts tell him I'll call him later'. There are two extra benefits to this; firstly, your callers get a human being to speak to, and secondly, you can do some quick prioritization before starting your call-back session. It may be in some instances that your colleague can answer the query on your behalf.

When you are pushed for time, you can cut the callers short politely.

You are probably already better at techniques for getting rid of people than you think – we all build up a stock of phrases and probably use them unwittingly when we are busy and need to get on:

■ 'Look, I'm sorry to interrupt you, but I'm really pressed for time at the moment…'
■ 'To be honest, it may be better if we saved this discussion until later, so that I've had a chance to think a bit more carefully about the issues…'

Two bonus tips are that if you want to stop someone in mid-flow, say their name: 'John, that's really interesting but…', and if you get really desperate, the universal way to signal you've had enough is to say the word 'anyway'. It'll stop even the most talkative person in their tracks.

The truth about… how to use voicemail

You'll have seen the merits of other technological advances discussed elsewhere in this book but it seems there's not much debate about voicemail – it's awful but we have to live with it.

This section is about doing just that with the least pain, inconvenience and heartache as possible. Although not instantaneous, voicemail can be a two-way exchange (on those days when you keep missing each other), so remember to look at it in terms of inbound and outbound communication.

It's important too to note that if you get it wrong at your end, you may be missing vital incoming messages – you'll never know how many people hung up, just because you got the outgoing message wrong!

Why did voicemail seem like a good idea?

■ It means we can 'answer' the phone when we're not around.
■ Callers get to hear a personal message from us.
■ We can manage our time better.
■ We can pick up messages remotely, so we don't need to return to the office.
■ Callers save time and frustration by not having to call back.
■ Callers can be sure that we'll actually get their message.
■ Messages can be left out of normal office hours for action the following day.

All of this sounds fine, and if voicemail wasn't so badly abused by the majority of users it would probably be judged as a good thing to have, a useful addition to the 'communications toolbox'.

When people ring, the thing they really want to do is to talk to you in person – it's you who can solve their problem, offer advice or help out. If you're not around then they would probably rather talk to someone who works with you, maybe someone who performs the same role. That would probably mean that they'd get some kind of an answer to their query. You might need to follow up at a later time to finalize details.

Next in the order of merit is the 'human message taker' – that is, someone who is able to say that you are not at your workplace but who will pledge to make sure that the message is delivered.

At the bottom of the list comes voicemail.

The truth about... voicemail technique
The dos

Listen to some other people's outgoing message and you come away not knowing if or when they will ever return your call. Here's some advice on how to handle your outgoing message and what to include:

■ *Your name* – if they've not spoken to you before, how can they be sure they're through to the right person?

■ *Your company* – especially if you have a phone system that allows outside callers to dial your phone direct. If they've dialled incorrectly at least they'll know they're through to the wrong organization!

■ *The date* – you should change your message every day – at least callers then know that you haven't disappeared for a three-month round-the-world trip. It has the added dimension of making you appear more efficient. If you are going on holiday then different rules apply (see below).

■ *A brief description of your movements* – with the emphasis on brief. You are trying to manage expectation. If you are going to be out all day then say so, then people won't be expecting a call back within the hour. If you will be in and out of meetings all day then say so – callers are then unlikely to keep ringing back to try to get you.

■ *A brief alternative* – be careful with this one as it can backfire. If you have a colleague who has agreed to pick up and sort out your calls then leave an alternative extension. Don't leave alternative contact numbers unless you can be sure they will deliver a result, so putting your mobile number on, when you know you'll be tied up with it switched off most of the day, will only increase your caller's frustration.

Voice – how to say it

■ *Talk fast* – at least faster than normal. This will get the message over quicker and increase the sense of enthusiasm in your voice. A slow dirge of a message will leave people with the impression that you're never very keen about being in work.

- *Use a standard message* – change the details every day, but keep the message in a format that you're used to. This will mean that when you dictate it, it will flow naturally and without interruption.
- *Speak clearly* – pay some attention to your diction; don't run words together or mumble. If you do, people will have no idea when you'll call them back and in some instances they may begin to hope you won't bother.
- *Just before you start your message, inhale deeply.* You should be able to dictate the whole thing without breathing in and out again. If not then it's probably too long. This is a good way of keeping the message 'clean'.
- *Sound enthusiastic* – plenty of rise and fall in your voice is much better than a dull monotone. Try to picture the caller as someone you like and be genuinely sorry to have missed their call.
- *Always listen to it back* – make sure you haven't clipped the start or end of the message or left too much space before the tone. Few people like the way they sound on voicemail, but try to be objective. If you were a big customer ringing up, what impression would the message you've just recorded convey? Is this someone you'd like to do business with? If the answer's no, then re-record it.

The don'ts

- *Don't waffle* – you have already 'upset' your caller by not being there, so it's unlikely they'll want to hear a long message about how busy you are and why you can't take the call in person. Be businesslike but friendly.
- *Don't leave a messed-up message* – If you get it wrong in any way at all then re-record it. This includes tone of voice, uncertainty about what you're saying, umming and erring or the background noise of colleagues shouting across the office.
- *Don't try to be funny* – Flippant remarks, sarcasm, even a sly dig at your company are all out. Your immediate peers might find all of this highly amusing, but it's less likely that one of your customers will! Even if your message is

genuinely funny, they won't be laughing at it in three months when they've heard it a dozen times.

■ *Don't use someone else to record it* – You'll simply look like you don't care who calls you – a personalized message is much better.

■ *Don't use voicemail unless you have to* – Switching it on as a way of vetting incoming calls is a really bad idea. Most people will soon work out you're doing this, which means that whenever they hear your voicemail message they'll think that you're available but not willing to speak to them. Apart from anything else, most successful business communication comes from listening and talking so it's plain stupid to try to cut it out.

■ *Don't apologize too much* – a lot of grovelling about not being around and how sorry you are that voicemail is the only alternative just wastes more time. These days we're all aware that this technology isn't perfect, but it does have its place.

Example 1 – A good daily message

'Hi, you're through to Hazel Bloom at The Inn on the Green, on Wednesday November 5th. I'm sorry I'm not around to take your call; you can either leave me a message or try me on my mobile, which is 01234 567 89, that's 01234 567 89. And thanks for your call.'

Example 2 – A good holiday message

'Hi, you're though to Hazel Bloom at The Inn on the Green – I'm away now until Thursday 20th November. If your call is urgent ring Tricia Hughes on 01234 678 45, that's 01234 678 45, or you can leave me a message and I'll get back to you on my return. And thanks for your call.'

Try this

You can learn a lot from how other people use voicemail.

Make a point of really stopping and listening hard every time you hear a voicemail message, then answer these three questions:

■ How well informed am I? Do I think it's worth ringing back? Do I think they'll ring me back? If so, when?

- How do I feel? Does the other party come across as keen and enthusiastic? Did it sound as if they cared about missing my call?
- What sort of communicator are they, efficient and passionate or lazy and unconcerned?

New technology always has a big 'wow' factor attached to it, but we soon get use to it and it becomes a part of everyday life. Once we start to take it for granted there is a danger we'll become complacent about how we use it, so remember that voicemail can be an asset or a liability; the balance of power lies in how you use it.

The truth about... outbound calls

We've looked at some methods of dealing with the unpredictability of inbound calls, which should help you take control and manage both your time and the calls themselves more efficiently.

Although a conversation still ensues with an outbound call, it's different in terms of the level of control you have. Check back with the list of differences at the start of the previous section and you'll see again how outbound calls give you the initiative.

This section is split into two, dealing separately with first calls, ie people you've never spoken to before, and then familiar calls. The latter category could be huge and embrace everything from old friends to a supplier you've dealt with only a few times before, but the same principles should apply.

First calls

First calls can be critical in establishing the future success, or otherwise, of any business relationship, so here are some tips on how to gain and keep the initiative with an initial call.

Before you launch into a monologue about the reason for your call you need to establish that you have got hold of the right person. That's okay if you've been given the name of an individual to contact, by a reliable source, about a specific issue, but if not you need to find out quickly.

This is a good discipline for preparing yourself. Before you even think about picking up the receiver you need to have thought through the objective of your call. Now this isn't difficult if you are calling to book a rail ticket, but if your boss has asked you to find a supplier of high-end graphic design services then you'll need to take more time to prepare.

Once you've made the connection and are talking to the right person you need to check to see how you're getting on in engaging with the person you're speaking to. This is a skill that will improve with time as long as you stay conscious of the need to do it.

You can use short phrases to do this, like 'Am I on the right lines here?', 'Is this the sort of thing you do?', 'Is this something you think you could help with?'

Even with a first call, if you engage quickly there can be a mix of social and business chat; just be careful that you don't overplay this

You need to keep your wits about you to spot the end of the call coming – you don't want the other party to put the phone down thinking that they were never going to get away from you (by the way, if they resort to using the 'anyway' word you know you've blown it).

Either keep complete control, do whatever business needs to be done and get out while the going is good, or be sensitive to them making 'closing' statements, like a summary of what you've said, or an attempt to agree the next stage of your transaction.

You may want to check back one final time, to make sure that they have got what they needed from the conversation.

Those key points again are as follows:

- Prepare to an appropriate level.
- Is this the right person?
- Listen for signs of their mood.
- Check back often.
- Listen for 'closing' signals.
- Make a final check back to clarify that a definite outcome has been reached.

Familiar calls

The upside of this kind of call is that it is generally much easier to manage; you stand a better chance of being able to govern the length, subject matter and tone of the call with a known person than a stranger.

The downside is that over-familiarity can easily creep in, which can result in long rambling chats about anything but the subject in hand. As we say above, it's a question of balancing social and business chat to get the best result in any set of circumstances.

Being too businesslike and never having time for small talk can be quite intimidating and might leave the other party feeling they've been snubbed in some way. Unadulterated gossip, with no business discussion whatever, will make them wonder how you ever get any work done!

Clearly we have to be sensitive to the needs of individuals. Some like to exchange pleasantries before getting down to business, others are less inclined to do so; the only rule here is to listen out for signals and make mental notes of the different personalities you deal with.

It's okay, too, to make notes (mental or otherwise) about their interests, the names of their children or other such details, so that you have some common ground in future conversations, but beware of overplaying this or you'll end up looking shallow!

The last thing to remember about outbound calls is that you can use them as a key element of your time management. If you make a prioritized list, you can govern the time of day and duration of many of your outbound calls (if you're not yet in the habit of doing this, then there's some great advice in Part 3, later on).

Mostly, you'll be able to govern the time of the call, so try to apply some sensible criteria. Make important calls in the morning when you are most attentive – save routine ones for the afternoon.

If you have to make a lot of calls that require the same output (say you're trying to arrange appointments), then make them all in one block; it's like applying the production line technique.

Use calls that have lighter subject matter (to a close colleague or friend) as a reward, and schedule them in for when you've finished writing that heavyweight report.

The truth about... meetings

I think meetings are a good opportunity to listen, but they have to be action orientated too, otherwise they just become talking shops.

Chris Major – AstraZeneca

Business meetings have become one of our primary methods of communication and they can take many forms. How useful any individual meeting is will depend on your role, your control and your expectation.

Here are some of the meetings you might be involved with:

■ a regular team briefing to let everyone know about (and discuss) the issues of the day/week;
■ a one-to-one meeting with your immediate boss to discuss a project you are working on or to set objectives for the coming weeks;
■ a get-together with a customer to discuss the possibility of a new order, or ways of improving service to them;
■ a brainstorming meeting to generate new ideas to solve problems.

How to prepare for meetings

If you come out of a meeting bored, frustrated or simply angry at the lack of any tangible action then some of it might be down to how well you prepared. Equally, it may also be due to the dull, bombastic, egotistical or plain stupid people who were in the meeting with you, but we can't solve all the problems of the world at once.

It's much more likely that the outcome will be positive if you take just a short time to prepare yourself before you enter the fray. The starting point for this will be to consider what the meeting is for. You'd be surprised at the number of people who turn up not knowing this and that lack of clarity helps to drag meetings down to the lowest common denominator.

When you know the reason for the meeting you can assess your role, and a few seconds' thought will also tell you how much prep time you should put in.

If you look in your diary and see 'Weekly sales performance update', then you might be interested but have little input (other than your listening skills). If, however, it's time for 'Annual performance appraisal', on which your future promotion and financial prospects depend, it might just be worth taking a bit more time out to prepare, yes?

Now consider who the meeting is with. There are two factors to think about, firstly the number of people and secondly their status. If it's an internal meeting, are these people your peers, your staff, the board of management?

External meetings might be with customers, suppliers or the general public and will require a different type of preparation.

Answering the question 'who' will point you towards how much control you're likely to have. A client meeting, at their premises, to an agenda that they've drawn up is unlikely to leave you much room for manoeuvre, but at least take the time to read what's going to be discussed so that you have an opinion, or in the worst-case scenario, a defence.

According to...

Chris Major – AstraZeneca

> I used to attend meetings run by a very senior civil servant who would come with the draft minutes already prepared, which was his attempt to be clear about the conclusions he wanted.
>
> With every item he'd just scribble a few changes to the draft that he'd made to capture the discussion that had gone on around the table, and he would actually conclude each item with 'well, would you all agree that we have decided this?'
>
> Once you knew he was doing it that way, my goodness, the meetings used to roll along! I wouldn't recommend that for everybody but it is an interesting approach.

This looks like a bit too much control for our liking, but it's probably true that if you can govern the pace and content of the discussion, you're much more likely to get your own way.

If you're in a meeting where you have only limited control, you'll need to think carefully about the timing of your input.

While we're on the subject of minutes, you need to agree with the parties to a meeting an appropriate level of detail. Sometimes it's wise to have detailed minutes taken of everything that's been said, but most meetings are less formal than this.

Still, it's tempting to not bother at all and the end result is that meetings become much less effective. At the very least you need a list of action points, a name against each and a date by when they must be completed. If you're chairing a meeting it's a good idea to sum up with this list at the end, so that everyone is clear what they have to do before you next get-together.

The truth about... when to contribute

Having done all your preparation for a meeting it's tempting to steam in at top speed when your particular agenda items arise. If a controversial topic is up for debate and you know that others will probably have the opposite viewpoint to you, there are times when it's good to state your case first, particularly if you have a persuasive argument that is hard to counter.

But it's often the case that we find issues that are more finely balanced, and in these situations it is no bad thing to sit back and listen to what others have to say first. This gives you the opportunity to assess the strength of feeling in the room, to work out who is on which side and who is open to persuasion, and it allows you the time to amend your own arguments before you open your fat stupid mouth.

According to...

Simon Terrington – Human Capital

> Be aware of the power of listening. Usually the more senior a person is at a meeting, the less they'll talk and the more they'll listen.

Really effective persuasion is about weighing all the factors carefully, then constructing your messages in a way that they're likely to gain maximum acceptance. Sometimes it really is only fools who rush in.

Celtic passion

An enthusiastic Welsh manager became well known for his impassioned outbursts during meetings. He could deliver an emotional soliloquy on virtually any subject, often setting himself up as the champion of the underdog.

On first seeing this happen his colleagues were awe struck, when he'd finished they broke out into spontaneous applause.

Sadly, further investigation revealed that although the passion burned like an inferno in his very soul, there was little to match it inside his head. In fact, there was rarely, if ever, a logical argument to back what he said, and if challenged with 'well, what practical steps do you think we should take to make things better?' he had to confess that he had no idea!

We would always advocate that passion is the best weapon in the communicators' armoury, but always remember that substantive argument is a good thing to have too!

How long to prepare?

There's no set of rules that governs how long you spend preparing, it's a question of judgement. What will help to guide you, though, is expectation. Think about what you want from the meeting and then put yourself in the shoes of the other party.

You might not see a routine meeting with one of your own team as that important, but for them it could be critical – are they working on a project that's reached a difficult stage? Do they need help with problem solving? Is there friction with other members of the team? These issues may well be unknown to you in advance, but if you are at least aware of how important this get-together is for the other party you will be more prepared to listen patiently and work together towards a solution.

Finally, it's always a good idea to check where the meeting is to be held. This is important for the obvious reason that you don't want to turn up at the wrong place!

Chauffeur driven

A middle manager at the BBC had been invited to attend a briefing to be held by the Director General. Although unsure of how she'd ended up on the guest list (most of the other managers due to attend were much more senior), she nevertheless set off in plenty of time.

Arriving at Broadcasting House in central London she made her way up the main stairwell towards the boardroom, where she thought the meeting was due to take place. Who should pass her on the way down but the Director General.

'Excuse me,' she said, 'but I was coming to your meeting, isn't it in the boardroom?' Politely he explained that it wasn't even in the same building, but as he was being chauffeured across town to Marylebone High Street (the real venue) perhaps he could offer her a lift.

They arrived at the correct destination to find that the fire alarm had gone off and all the senior managers had been evacuated and were standing on the pavement outside. How they all gasped when the chauffeur opened the door and let out first the DG and then her!

Where a meeting is being held can also be a vital part of a successful outcome because the surroundings can change the dynamic of the meeting in a dramatic fashion.

According to...

Professor David Clutterbuck

Look at the space and environment for your discussion. A practical example was a Chief Executive who I was working with who could not get her top team of managers to be open with her.

She said that communications around the table were difficult. I asked her 'which table' and she said 'this one'. And it was the table in her office. So we asked 'what do you think having all the meetings in your office is saying, and how is that affecting the quality of the communications?'

She changed the location and suddenly, bingo! Everyone started opening up.

How useful was that?

The point of the story centres around territory. Very often people's surroundings and environment can affect their behaviour, especially when it comes to their willingness to contribute their opinion. In this example, choosing a more neutral venue put people at their ease and they were consequently far more willing to join in.

The truth about... post-meeting afterglow

It's tempting after a long meeting to find some means of escape. You might rush back to your workstation and start on the e-mail backlog; alternatively, you may head for the canteen for a coffee or out of the back door for a cigarette.

Very few people take the time to think what they've learnt from a meeting. When it's all over, ask yourself these questions:

- What did I learn?
- What did I 'teach'?
- What did we decide?
- What did we create?
- What did we exchange?

The reason for these questions is that they are fundamental to the success of all meetings. Did I hear anything new or tell the rest of the participants something they didn't already know? Collectively, did we take any action that will help us, either through reaching an agreement about something or by pooling our collective knowledge and creativity?

What it eventually boils down to is: what did I take to the meeting and what did I bring back from it? What the hell was the point of it all?

Just a short time reflecting on this will give you an objective picture of whether or not the meeting was useful and that in itself will help you in planning for the next one.

The truth about... presentations

Forget all the scare stories about public speaking and presentations; it's really easy when you get the hang of it. That doesn't mean you won't be nervous and a little uncomfortable before the start of it, but remember that the applause of an appreciative audience is the kind of instant gratification that it's hard to find elsewhere.

If you keep the end point in mind, it will help steer your preparation and give you a much better chance of being a success.

Attention span – what we can learn from the goldfish

So, they say that every time the goldfish swims round the bowl is like a fresh experience; it simply can't remember that it's been there before.

There's plenty of evidence to suggest that we are becoming increasingly goldfishian as time goes by. Broadcast media are a great reflection of this. There is an ongoing policy of sign-posting so that we always know what's coming up next and this is often interspersed with references to what we are currently tuned to, just in case we've forgotten.

Who let the DOGS out?

Most satellite TV channels now carry digital on-screen graphics (DOGS), as a reminder of the station we are tuned to. These normally appear in the corner of the screen, often with a slightly translucent quality that means we can see the programme behind them. In a multi-channel environment, where much of the content we see is a repeat of 'classics' from long ago, each TV network feels the need to remind viewers who has brought them this gem.

We can learn from the world of television if we need to put together a presentation.

When you are faced with keeping your audience engaged there are three ways of doing it:

■ expectation
■ content
■ style.

Expectation – if you tell your audience up front about what's on the menu then there is a chance they will stay with you, but there's a catch. You have to get content and style right too. So, for example, if you manage their expectation by saying 'For the next hour I am going to explain to you our order processing system in fine detail, using no visual aids, no audience participation and in a dull monotone voice', then you may have told them what to expect but they'll hardly feel engaged.

There's only one way of making the above scenario worse and that's not to warn them at all. Under those circumstances they'll be bored and they'll resent you forever!

Even with difficult, tedious detail, most audiences will stick with you if you're prepared to explain why and how you intend to present the information.

So, a better start would be:

> During the next hour I need to explain our order processing system so we can open the debate about how to make it better.
>
> I'll start with a quick graphic showing the 10 steps of the process – then spend a couple of minutes going through each one. I'll also give you the input of our production team and a customer panel at each stage, so you'll get an idea of how well the process serves us and what it delivers, or fails to deliver, to customers.

The whole issue of managing expectation is vital if you are to succeed.

According to...

Alistair Smith – Alite

> Draw attention throughout to what it is you're doing and explain not only the content but your thinking behind it. Keep the audience focused on the content and don't present yourself as an authority figure. A lot of people make that mistake – 'listen to me because I'm an expert', but then you're into a dog fight, it's a challenge to prove you are as good as you say you are.

Professor David Clutterbuck gives his thoughts on what contributes towards a successful presentation.

The expert panel

David Clutterbuck – University professor

The first thing is not to get in the way of the message. One of the first lessons I was taught was to look at how you dress and not to wear bright-coloured socks, for example, because they distract people, and not to have too many overheads because again it distracts people from the message.

Make it easy for people to listen to you and that means not standing behind a podium unless you can help it – get out among them and always think about it as a conversation.

If I think about giving a lecture it always gets stilted, but if I think about having a conversation with people then it's much easier and that doesn't matter if I'm with a thousand people or four people.

That means I spend a lot of time listening to them as well – you really need to interact with your audience from the very first point.

The amount of information they absorb is much higher if they've had some engagement in its construction, so instead of putting up a load of slides and reading them out, I would get them to talk about what's on the slides.

Often you'll know what an audience wants to hear but if you engage them then they'll tell you – there's no argument about it then.

David Clutterbuck is a well-established and extremely competent speaker, though by his own admission much of this has come about because he has worked hard on his technique.

If his advice looks hard to follow, it's because this kind of skill only comes with practice, but at least it gives us something to aspire to.

The truth about... managing PowerPoint

Because it is so widely used in presentations, we thought it was necessary to devote a section to the use of PowerPoint as an aid to presentation. We've already said that before you've even put up your first slide it's a good idea to manage the expectation of your audience, as that way they're less likely to drift off to sleep.

If you have a small number of slides, say so at the start. 'I just want to run you through a short PowerPoint presentation to illustrate my case, it's actually only half a dozen slides and it'll take about 15 minutes.'

If you have a medium number of slides then put the number of the slide on each, so as the slide comes up it'll say 'number 1 of 20' and so on, giving the audience the chance to assess how long is left.

If you have a large number of slides then break it down into more manageable pieces. Again it helps if you are up front. 'Okay, there are about 60 slides to go through but they're in three distinct sections: where are we now?, where do we want to be? and how do we get there?' (A lovely list of three!) 'We'll just be spending 10 minutes on each section as there are quite a lot of graphs and illustrations and that should leave us enough time to debate the issues that arise.'

This might seem like sound advice but to be honest none of it will do you any good at all if you misuse the tool. Technique is all-important.

According to...

Professor Cary Cooper

> What is really bad from a communication point of view is when someone puts a PowerPoint presentation up and reads each of the 12 things on each of the 12 slides in slow time.
>
> I just flash the slide up and pick out a couple of points then move on, I think you shouldn't leave any slide up for more than 45 seconds.
>
> I'd also avoid doing numbered lists because people are waiting for the next point; it's much better if it's non-linear because you then have the flexibility to make the points you want without being tied into some kind of chronology that doesn't work.

As with all technology, there are risks that the equipment will let you down and sometimes this can happen at the most critical point of your address. It's a good idea to have a contingency plan if you can.

According to...

Simon Terrington – Human Capital

> When I do a big presentation I have paper prints of the slides and distribute them to the audience, so if it crashes you can just say, 'turn to page 6 on the document in front of you' and you can keep going. Of course, you can only do that with 20 people, you can't do it with 200.

It's never a good idea to give out paper prints at the start of a presentation though, as people will tend to skip ahead rather than listen to what you're saying. In the case of a sales pitch, the greatest likelihood is that they'll be on the last page (where the pricing information usually appears) before you're halfway through the first slide.

Top tips for using PowerPoint effectively:

■ Try to keep the number of slides as few as possible; remember they are a bulleted form of your presentation – not the whole thing!
■ Manage your audience's expectation – let them know how many slides you're using right at the start.
■ Keep text simple – don't clutter your slides with too many bullet points and never use blocks of text.
■ Think of slides like poster advertisements – how much information do they fit on a hoarding? Your slides should contain no more.
■ Use pictures – graphic illustrations can make a point better than words, especially if you animate the slide.
■ Keep it pacey – don't leave one slide up for too long; remember the 45-second rule.

In this chapter we've dealt with many of the most commonly used tools of communication. All of these technologies were developed to help us make our daily interaction more effective, but it's easy for the opposite to apply, if the tools are used badly.

The elevator test for Chapter 9

Listening and talking are vital components of good relationships – they are at the core of communication.

Apply strict criteria to incoming phone calls to assess how vital they are to your working day and then manage them appropriately.

Manage your outbound calls and plan them effectively – don't snatch up the handset and dial without thinking.

Pay special attention to 'first calls' – they're the starting point for new relationships.

How productive meetings are is often governed by your role, your control and your expectation.

Not all meetings are of equal importance – allocate your planning time accordingly.

If you're presenting to an audience, engage them with expectation, content and style.

PowerPoint is immensely powerful – in the right hands!

10

Feeling

The truth about... non-verbal communication

Introduction

If it really were true that what you see is what you get we wouldn't need this next section. But because we are human and complex, there are loads of non-verbal signals that we transmit and receive all the time which contribute to the understanding of the messages that are passed between us.

Frankly, we don't always say what we mean. You can see this happening a lot during courtship, which is sometimes described as a dance between two people. Often it is the unsaid that communicates the most.

We're going to take a look at some of the most common forms of non-verbal communication and try to understand what the signals mean, so that we can better manage what we're transmitting through our actions and understand more of what other people are 'saying' to us through their deeds rather than their words.

The truth about... first impressions

Sir John Hall, the businessman behind The Metro Centre and Newcastle Football Club, was once asked how long it took him to assess a company he was dealing with when he visited their premises. 'A matter of seconds' was his typically blunt reply. His view is further supported by one of our panel of experts.

According to...
Professor Chris Brewster

> The research tells us quite clearly that people form an impression literally within about 20 seconds, and there is very little you can do, after that, to change that impression – you fight it from then on, or reinforce it.
> I think a lot of communicators don't think seriously enough about that, so they start their conversation with 'ah, well, errm, like errm, sort of err, it's nice to be here sort of thing' and if that's the first impression that people get, then it really is bad news, so I really believe that first impressions are one of the key moments of truth.

When we encounter other individuals for the first time we do the same and although we occasionally get it wrong, more often than not our instincts are correct, based on a mixture of experience and intuition.

As this is a 'gift' we share with most of humankind, we can be pretty sure that they are making the same judgements about us, so what can we do to make the best first impression?

One to one
Preparation and planning are key elements when you're out to make a good impression. To do your current job you probably had to go through some sort of selection interview, so you should have considered many of these things already.

Appearance
If you're the type of person who doesn't take much time to go clothes shopping and even less wondering what goes with what, then you're probably a man over the age of 35.

Stop thinking that it's not important – you don't have to dress in an Armani suit, but you do have to look like you've made the effort. Have your best shoes seen better days? Does your suit look like a throwback to a previous decade? Well, it's time to smarten up.

It's equally important for men and women to be conscious of how they appear to others. Don't let anyone else tell you how to present yourself, but do ask the advice of someone you trust, after you've chosen your desired look. It's important to remember that you are presenting a first impression of you, not a catalogue model or a shop dummy. When you're happy with the way you look it's far more likely that you'll relax quickly and be yourself and that helps you to show your best side.

When you look in the mirror, try to see yourself from someone else's point of view – don't go against type and try shock tactics with a bright flowery dress or a big hat unless you'd dress like that anyway – and if you do, remember that most people prefer surprises to shocks, so tone it down until they've got to know you a bit better.

The golden rule is to be comfortable, both physically in terms of the fit of your clothes and emotionally with regard to how you feel about yourself, when you're dressed this way.

Grooming is important too; maybe the length and style of your hair doesn't fit in with everyone's idea of what is conventional, but that's less important than keeping it clean. Every now and then, take a conscious look round at how other people look – you don't have to follow the trend, but be aware of what it is.

Finally, make-up should follow the same rule as perfume/ aftershave. Across the board you should aim for subtlety, especially with fragrances; after all, once you've left the meeting room you want your aura to remain, not your aroma.

How do I look?

In the hyper-competitive eighties, the photocopying business was as ruthless as any. The organizations at the top of the pile were typified by a macho culture, where communication was very direct and the 'will to win' extremely strong.

Under these circumstances virtually anything could be seen as an area of competitive advantage over other players in the market. At the foot of the stairs of a regional office of Rank Xerox was a full-length mirror, which no salesperson could avoid seeing on their way out – above it was printed, 'Would you buy from this man?'

How do I look too?

A spiteful press will always try to find ways of criticizing a politician whose views they don't share. In Liverpool in the 1980s, one such leading figure was Derek Hatton. Not content with disagreeing with his political views, some papers sought to undermine him by criticizing his fastidious personal grooming and taste in clothes, which included expensive suits. At the time they printed a story saying that the mirror in Hatton's office bore the legend, 'Yes Derek, you do look brilliant!'

The truth about... behaviour
Be yourself

At least be the most acceptable version of yourself under the circumstances. That means, until you've had the opportunity to 'explore' the other party, and vice versa, it's best to be a little cautious. Over-familiarity too soon can be very threatening.

According to...

Simon Terrington – Human Capital

> There's some interesting work been done on intimacy which is that if I meet you for the first time and I hardly know you, and we're having a bit of a chat, and I say by the way I've got VD, you'd be absolutely shocked because I've jumped to a level of intimacy that you just don't want to be at.
>
> Whereas if we start off slowly and we become friends and I say in a spirit of confidentiality and concern that I've got it, then it's something you can deal with and support me. But to get to those levels of intimacy people have to offer the same back until you go deeper and deeper. It has to be a balance.

It's also true that if you consciously want to get closer to someone, a starting point is to reveal something personal about yourself (though not as personal as in the example above). Under normal circumstances, this will lead them to trade a similar piece of information in return.

The truth about... body language

Body language burst onto the popular business behaviour scene in the 1970s, and hundreds of books appeared about it, to the point that it has become a bit of a cliché.

For a while it was the secret skill, which we could learn and use to transmit all kinds of messages to other people without them ever understanding our 'magic'.

It was also hailed as the route to discovering what the other party wanted, without them ever saying it, like a secret way into their soul.

We think that you should be aware of body language and its significance; you should know, on a conscious level, what different signs mean and where possible you should be sensitive to the signals the other party is sending out (there is a very good chance that you are already expert at this on a subconscious level).

As far as 'controlling' your own body language to send out only the signals you choose is concerned, it's worth noting that there is a limit to what you can do. In a stress or conflict situation, for example, you are more likely to adopt a closed position (see below) and making a conscious effort to change your posture is only likely to last for a short time before you revert to type. With practice and concentration you can master some of your actions, but it will always be a struggle.

Instead, you should put your efforts into changing the way that you feel, in effect tracing your body language (the outward manifestation of feelings) back to the source. Once you've learnt to manage your feelings, your body language will fall into line behind.

According to...

Alistair Smith – Alite

> You've only got the one body and you've developed a set of mannerisms, a way of walking, a way of standing that all your life has been invested in, so it's difficult to undo that.
>
> There are certain superficial things that you can alter and undo, so if when you're doing a presentation you jangle the

146 ■ How to...

change in your pocket because you're nervous then take it out before you start and the problem is half way to being solved.

But overall the theory that body follows mind holds true, so what you tend to get is non-verbal leakage.

What that means is that if mentally you're in anguish then physiologically your body reflects that in high anxiety; you literally leak, you perspire and that's how they measure lies on lie detectors.

The truth about... the key elements of body language

Here are some simple things you can look out for to give you clues about the way people are feeling:

■ *Eye contact* – often described as the window to the soul, the eyes can give away a lot about what the other party is thinking. Sometimes though, the signs can be open to misinterpretation. Eye contact can signal attraction, or it can be very threatening. For that reason you have to read it along with other things, like tone of voice or stance.

If someone makes sustained eye contact with you over a candlelit dinner you can imagine the kind of signal that might send. On the other hand, if the eye contact is from a mugger in the street who is demanding money with menace you may well feel differently.

■ *Body posture* – a 'closed' position might be sitting hunched with arms folded and legs crossed and naturally looks defensive. However, this could be caused by a whole series of emotions, maybe guilt over having not done something, simply being nervous in the present company or possibly secretive about sensitive information – they all look the same, but may require different approaches to get the other party to relax.

The contrary 'open' position, feet apart, arms loosely at sides, sitting upright, suggests the very opposite. This is someone who's in control of the situation and relaxed about it. They're far more likely to be ready to indulge in an open exchange of views.

- *Mirroring* – this is the behaviour that people undertake when they want the other party to like them. It is most stark when observed amongst courting couples. In an attempt to show approval for the other person we match our gestures and movements to theirs. As one party picks up their drink, so the other follows a fraction of a second later. What we can learn from this is that if someone is mirroring us, they like us – that's something you'll find useful when trying to get your message across.
- *Frowning with fists clenched* – this is a sure sign that you are about to be punched very hard.

According to...

Simon Terrington – Human Capital

> Mirroring is really interesting and if you analyse good sales people they really mirror the blinking and the facial twitches and all the actions of the person they're talking to and they have this incredible ability that is totally to do with empathy.

The breakdown of a relationship can be very stressful and harsh exchanges of words can often be accompanied by non-verbal communication that's equally challenging.

John Akers has been mediating between couples for many years, often bringing both parties together in the same room for the first time since the split. This is the sort of thing he has witnessed.

The expert panel

John Akers – A Relate Counsellor

I see a range of facial expressions. Other important non-verbal cues are chair positioning, playing with your hands, not having eye contact or alternatively having quite fierce eye contact, being intent on writing notes, this sort of thing.

You see cases of people trying to avoid engaging personally either with the mediator or the ex-partner, or even the opposite, trying to woo the mediator onto their side, and some women can be very adept at that and use their sexual powers to what they hope will be great advantage.

The smiles and the leg crossing I think may not be entirely unintentional.

Try this

Take half an hour out to do some people watching. Find a busy coffee bar in town and note down what you observe (but don't make it too obvious!).

What first impression do people make on you, and is that altered when you hear them speak or see what they order?

Watch out for people meeting up – how do they greet each other? What does it tell you about each of them, about their relationship? By their body language, do they look like friends or work colleagues? What is the balance of power between them?

Look around; who seems relaxed and comfortable, who looks tense or stressed? What do you think might be causing it? This is a great way of coming to understand the finer points of non-verbal communication and makes you think much harder about the effects your actions have on others, before you've even uttered a word.

The truth about... touching

Some cultures like touching, in southern Europe to hold someone by the arm just shows you're engaging with them, whereas if you're in Scandinavia that might be seen as being close to an assault.

Professor Chris Brewster

An important issue related to body language is touching. We're not talking about full-on hugging, just a light gesture like a hand in the small of the back as you go through into a meeting, or the leaning across and squeezing of a forearm to show a connection.

As Chris Brewster points out in his opening remarks, the problem with touching is that it can be very open to misinterpretation. It is something that doesn't work well across cultures.

According to...

Simon Armson – Samaritans

The other thing you have to take account of is culture; the British are fairly undemonstrative, but some of the Latin races are far more likely to touch.

It can be a good thing to confirm something that's important.

> The communication that comes from physical touching need not to be totally excluded, but it has to be carefully put into context in terms of appropriateness.

Even within a single culture our upbringing, social class and environment can have a profound effect on our willingness to touch or be touched:

■ Some men may feel uncomfortable being touched by women in case they wrongly interpret it as a sign of attraction.

■ In some circumstances men feel uneasy about being touched by other men, for fear of being seen as less macho.

■ Women may feel threatened by a man who is a frequent toucher, even if he appears not to be interested in them in other ways.

■ Fathers and sons often find it hard to touch or embrace, particularly during the 'teenage' years.

■ Teams involved in sport may find it easier to touch than other groups (they are usually well used to embracing after a goal has been scored!).

According to...

John Akers – a Relate Counsellor

> I think it's now more acceptable for a man to hug his son than it ever was and I think that's a good thing. Certainly I hug my own son, but I can't remember my father hugging me – I just think that's because things have changed.
>
> In the jargon you'd say that men are now a little more aware of their feminine side, which is a phrase that's always amused me because I don't see why it's a particularly feminine thing to touch.

Certainly within British culture it does look as though attitudes are changing, though we still have to be careful of the circumstances under which we consider touching as it can mean different things at different times.

According to...

Simon Armson – Samaritans

> It can mean all sorts of things and it depends entirely on the circumstances and the environment and the expectations and so on of the people concerned – it can be threatening, it can also be enabling, it can be supportive, it can be empathetic, it can communicate a degree of closeness that words wouldn't reach.

The truth about... culture

> *Culture is how people behave when they're not thinking about it.*
>
> Michael Angus – ex-chairman of Unilever

Culture has already come up, but why is it so important?

What we're trying to do is assess and monitor the effect of our surroundings on the way we communicate, because it's only if you can set your messages into some kind of relevant context that you'll stand any chance of them being well received.

There are two types of culture that we're going to look at here; one is the difference between nations, the other centred on organizations.

You may not have reached a stage in your career where you're hopping on and off planes as you sort out your company's problems around the world, but with the increasing global nature of business and the trend towards mixed race communities, you do need to be aware of how to cope with different cultures. Here are some tips on how to avoid getting it wrong:

■ *Read up* – if you know that you are going to be handling all incoming calls from your organization's office in Delhi, then either go to the library and get an appropriate book or do some Internet research that tells you about lifestyle, religion, custom and practice and even social norms.

■ *When in Rome* – try to adapt yourself to the other culture instead of expecting them to adapt to you. If you end up working in a multi-cultural environment (which is more and more likely these days), then be prepared to give ground and you'll soon find that people will respond, allowing you to find a compromise that suits both cultures.

According to...

Surinder Hundal – Nokia

> When I took my first trip to China I was only there for a week, during which I did three days of sightseeing and then two days of business because that is what I was expected to do – I was expected to know the country and the people before I sat down and engaged with them.
>
> That will not work in Finland, it's like come in and get stuck into business right away, so you have to pay attention to that kind of thing.

- *Be polite* – We doubt that there's any nation that is deliberately rude (oh, you can think of one!), but certainly in business some countries take a much more direct and focused approach than others and have little time for small talk. For the time being, it's much better to err on the side of courtesy, at least until you've come to terms with the work ethic of the other party.
- *Ask for feedback* – if you think you may have overstepped the mark or caused offence then politely ask if this is the case and apologize for your cultural ignorance. Most people will forgive most things if they believe it's a genuine mistake, but consistently serving bacon sandwiches when the Rabbi visits isn't likely to win you any friends in the Synagogue.

According to...

Lynn Rutter – Oxfam

> Once, when I was in a hotel in Kuala Lumpur I rang down and ordered a table for 7 o'clock please for room 327 and they said would you like a chair as well and I said of course thank you and was quite huffy that they were 'taking the Mickey'.
>
> But lo and behold at 7 o'clock, as I'm just about to leave my room, there's a knock on the door and in they came with

a table and chair, which they put down, bowed politely and went out, no doubt thinking 'stupid foreigner' and I'd been thinking 'stupid foreigner' – but it's an example that emphasizes your own cultural arrogance.

Of course I then had to ring down for room service.

As well as the obvious point that Lynn Rutter makes about cultural differences, there's an important lesson here too about the need for clarity in all the communications we make.

Watch and listen – rather than charging headlong into your new relationship, be a little more reserved and take the time to watch and listen. This is all the more valuable if you are alongside a colleague from the same background as yourself, who has had some experience of the culture you are integrating into.

The expert panel

Lynn Rutter – Oxfam

I didn't go to university and my first job was working as a tea trolley lady at Green Shield Stamps. It formed my communications skills in a great way, because I was working alongside glorious people like Annie and Flo and Gladys, who were the salt of the earth trolley ladies and I didn't want to come across as some stuck-up middle-class kid.

So you learn very fast to listen to people and pick up on what they're saying and communicate at the various levels that they need you to communicate at.

I don't mean that in any way to say that these people were not bright, but they didn't have an academic vocabulary so there was no point in talking on a highfalutin level, you had to talk to people about what you wanted them to do in a very straightforward and simple and plain and understandable way – and I guess that was a very good lesson.

You saw a lot of the office workers treating these people like they were dirt because they hadn't got a degree and they didn't go to the right school and they hadn't done the correct things and actually these people were far more passionate about what they did than the stuck-up office workers.

So you learnt very quickly that you have to adapt your style of communication, not expect them to adapt their level of understanding.

More and more companies are coming across the challenges of managing and communicating across different cultures as society in general becomes more mixed race and bigger organizations operate in many markets. Here we've talked about some of the subtleties of different cultures, but it's also worth noting that some things cut across all boundaries; fundamentals like respect, openness and courtesy are never out of place.

According to...

Bill Dalton – HSBC

> There are interesting cultural issues in managing global organizations; our experience is that while the cultures may vary, the people aren't that different.
>
> Bad communication is bad communication whether it's in the UK, in Canada, in the States, in France, in Asia, Brazil, it's no different, so the rules that apply in many cases apply because communication by definition involves people.
>
> They may have cultural differences, they may use chop sticks instead of knives and forks, but they're going to be just as annoyed if they hear about their boss leaving on an e-mail rather than someone having the common courtesy and respect to come down and tell them before they heard it like everybody else.

The truth about... organizational culture

Up until about 10 years ago no one talked much about organizational culture, maybe because we were all too busy living it.

Now it has become a modern obsession, as we become more introspective, both personally and commercially. Like all these fads, it has its good and it has its bad. Here's a summary of both sides:

■ Plus
  - Fosters greater understanding.
  - Keeps us more in touch.
  - We are better able to predict outcomes.
  - Our planning improves.
  - We have a clearer direction.

■ Minus
  - We become self-obsessed.
  - It wastes time.
  - The effect stifles creativity.
  - We are disempowered.
  - Complacency sets in.

So on the upside, when we know what makes the organization tick, we're better able to cope with the ups and downs of corporate life, we have a greater understanding of where we sit versus our competitors (presumably we've spent some time thinking about their culture too), and knowing ourselves makes us better able to perpetuate our culture going forward. This can be helpful if you think about things like recruitment. If you know the nebulous unspoken things that make the company the way it is, it becomes much easier to spot who will be able to adapt to the culture and who won't.

The opposite of all this results in an organization that is strangled by its own self-belief, that it is right in the face of evidence to the contrary. In recent years, we have seen examples of large companies, formerly at the top of their industry, fall from grace, for the simple reason that they convinced themselves that they had all the answers. There's an unnerving smugness about this kind of navel gazing that makes us all laugh when it results in a fall.

When it comes to the kind of blind faith that some organizational cultures perpetuate, it ends with new ideas being squashed and creativity stifled. People simply stop questioning the system.

See if the following anecdote makes you think of an organization you've worked for.

Monkey business

You take a cage and put five monkeys in it, then at one end of the cage you put a banana. Naturally the monkeys will run to the banana, but when they do you spray them with very cold water. Soon the monkeys learn not to run to the banana.

Then you replace one of the monkeys with a new monkey. When he gets in the cage he looks at the banana, then at the other four dumb monkeys and decides he'll run to the banana.

As he does so, all the other monkeys jump on him and beat him up because they don't want him to suffer like they did and get sprayed with cold water. Effectively they've learnt that the banana is out of bounds.

Over time you keep on replacing the old monkeys with new ones, until you have five brand new ones who've never been sprayed with water.

You ask any of those monkeys why they don't go to the banana and they'll tell you they don't know, it's just the way things are done around here.

The awful thing for many organizations is that having done all this navel gazing, they come to the conclusion that there are lots of things about themselves that they don't like and embark on a process of culture change – be warned, it's a long and difficult process and the changes that happen are only ever incremental.

Whatever the good and bad of all this, if you work for a big organization you'll be able to think of people who are counter-cultural. Either they're too aggressive in an over-polite culture, or they're not tough enough for an in-your-face culture. Inevitably what happens is that the culture wins and the individuals either adapt or leave – sad in some cases, but it's a fact of life.

When organizational cultures clash, there may be a need to find a creative solution to the problem.

The expert panel

Chris Brewster – University professor

There's a great story of when IBM took over Lotus Notes. There was a real clash of cultures because Lotus Notes was a pretty wild and creative place, where people would turn up in shorts and t-shirts when they felt like it and, in some cases, the guys even wore dresses, but as long as they were creating new and innovative packages no one really cared.

They got taken over by IBM, which is quite the opposite, and the guy from IBM stood up in front of all the people at Lotus and said how wonderful it was that they'd joined together and blah, blah, blah and someone in the audience said, 'We've got a free and easy culture here and would you ever consider coming to work in a dress?'

And his reply was: 'You hit the profit target I'm looking for and I'll come to work in a dress', which focused them on the financial bit that under normal circumstances they'd rather leave to someone else.

For the IBM guy it was clever because he wanted them to concentrate on the profit while at the same time making sure he didn't stifle their culture.

CASE STUDY

A COMPARISON OF CULTURES

Kay Winsper, Microsoft's Head of Great Company, high-lighted corporate cultures by contrasting the differences between her own organization and the *Financial Times* news-paper. What do you think would be the differences in communication style within the two organizations?

I did a job swap with Lucy Kellaway, a renowned journalist on the *FT*.

The main differences in culture between Microsoft and the *FT* were that Microsoft concentrates on teams, but the *FT* is built on individuals and the reward and recognition of individuals. They work on adrenaline on the deadlines, they don't have any processes in place at all other than a 10:30 meeting to decide the stories, the 11:30 meeting to decide the headlines, then you research till 4:30 and write the article with a 5:30 deadline.

Any of the journalists I met certainly didn't think about what the future holds. They're not concentrating on next week's article, it's very much about the now.

In terms of the environment, there was a wealth of infor-mation on everyone's desk, they were piled high, four deep, the only thing that you could see was the keyboard and even around their desks it was just extremely cluttered, but the clutter mattered — it was a totally different environment to Microsoft, but it works for them because you don't see the *FT* with blank pages the next day.

Our lesson from all of this is to not worry unduly about how you adapt your communication within your own organization (though you will naturally take account of who your audience is at any one time). Once you've worked for a company for a few weeks the culture will most likely be oozing out of your pores, you will know where the boundaries are and will not make the mistake of crossing them. What you have to be careful of is assuming that other organizations have the same culture as yours.

Pretty young things

Part of the tendering process for a major public sector catering contract involved potential suppliers doing a presentation about how they would handle day-to-day situations. A senior figure asked the following of one of the applicants.

'An overseas investor is visiting our office to see about setting up a new factory in the area, which is important for our economic development. I ring you to say we would like lunch laid on; what questions do you ask me?'

The caterer's reply started well.

'I'd ask what stage of the negotiation you were at and what you hoped to achieve from the day, then I'd suggest some way of having a theme at lunchtime that would help make the day memorable for your guests. So, if it was a formal sit-down meal we may supply a couple of waiters dressed as butlers.'

At this point the hapless fellow failed to realize the culture of equality and political correctness of the public sector. He buried his chances with the words… 'On the other hand, if it was less formal, maybe we'd have couple of pretty young waitresses in short skirts.'

In many organizations he'd have got away with it; we leave it up to you to decide if that's right or not, but his misjudgement of the culture he was in was most definitely wrong.

Try this

If you want to improve your empathy skill, that's to say your ability to see the world through other people's eyes, then take the time to step outside yourself by exploring other interests.

A good story

A very simple way to achieve this is to buy one magazine a month that you would normally never think of, so if you're a man choose a women's fashion magazine and vice versa. Alternatively, you could pick something that is outside your age range (teenage?), or a specialist interest publication (photography, flower arranging, showbiz gossip etc).

Take note of the articles and the advertisements to get a feel for how the average reader of this magazine sees life and don't forget to check out the letters page, for even greater insight.

Not only will you get a view on how other people think, but your speed of intuition will increase too.

The elevator test for Chapter 10

You only have a few seconds to make a first impression.

Clothes, grooming and cosmetics are all important factors.

Act naturally; it's you they want to see.

Your own non-verbal output is hard to control.

Learn to read the basics of eye contact, posture and mirroring.

Touching is risky but significant.

Make the effort to understand the cultures of different nations.

Knowing company culture can help with understanding but stifle creativity.

Be sensitive to the culture of other organizations you deal with.

Part 3

Planning for success

Some strategies for turning your intentions into actions

11

Planning

The truth about... preparing your personal communication plan

> You have to remember that no organization stands still, so if you yourself don't continually improve your own communication style, by default you will be moving backwards relative to your organization.
>
> Russell Grossman – BBC

Your personal communication strategy will need to be planned too if you are going to get any better, but isn't planning boring? Because of that we've developed a system that cuts down on the time, the pain and the frustration that goes with most planning exercises.

Why plan?

Most of the time we are living our lives *unconsciously* – we all are. That's to say we wake each morning and perform a routine of tasks; some domestic, some social, some work related and then we go to bed and start the cycle again.

Now and again, we snap out of this state to do an 'occasional' activity, like book a holiday or enjoy the Christmas break, but the older we get, the more times we've performed this task and it too becomes part of the cycle of routine, it just happens less often than brushing our teeth.

How often do you make enough time to sit down and really look at what's going on around you, to think about who you are and whether you're happy? Becoming conscious is the first step to breaking the routine and changing the status quo; only then can you start to take decisions about where you're going.

According to...

Jan Shawe – Sainsbury's

> I think people who've been around for a long time know how important it is to make conscious efforts to improve their communication but I think even then you have got to sort of almost diarize it, when was the last time I spoke to the team etc.
>
> At the beginning of the year I'll put in the diary that I want a weekly team meeting with my senior team just to make sure it really happens. Whilst it's an instinctive thing to do I still think it takes a bit of prior planning to make sure those dates and times are put in the diary and are sacred, because it's so easy to cancel things. So there's quite a lot of instinct there but then there's some actual nitty gritty of bog basic getting it in the diary and making sure it happens.

When you've finished planning and started to implement your new strategy you'll find you have so much more time for the things that matter. There's one law of physics that none of us can change – time is finite.

Joe's story

Back in the 1970s, before the days of sophisticated computer technology, most analysis in business had to be done in a painstaking way.

If, for the sake of argument, you wanted to know how many of your customers spent more than £100,000 a year with you, probably the best you could do would be to print out on massive sheets of interlinked computer pages (known as music paper) all the customer names and their expenditure to date.

Then someone (let's call him Joe) would have to go through line by line, picking out the names of the big spenders and writing them down on a separate sheet of paper. As the thirst for knowledge increased (it's the only way to stay ahead of the competition), Joe was asked to complete these tasks more and more frequently, until it became almost his whole job.

One day, a naive young subordinate of Joe asked 'Don't you get fed up each time the boss asks you to do another one of these exercises?' to which Joe replied 'Well, if I wasn't doing this, I'd be doing something else.'

That piece of distorted philosophy kept Joe going through the most tedious of tasks, but what it reinforces is the message that time is finite, and because of that it's a valuable resource that we should allocate with thought and care.

This is all the more relevant when you consider the 'information overload' that we all suffer from now. We simply have to be more selective about our communication inputs and outputs.

Why we fail

The big mistake we often make (and it causes us to fail) is that we embark on a programme of personal change management that's simply unachievable, over-ambitious or plain daft.

Self-improvement – January gym syndrome

There's no business more seasonal than the fitness industry. We calculate that a massive 60 per cent of new memberships are signed in the first two weeks of every year, brought about partly by our guilt feelings about over-indulgence and partly because of the opportunity a new year presents, for a fresh start.

Sadly this doesn't last. Statistically you are likely to attend the gym only 12 times before you let your membership lapse.

Take out the visit for your assessment, the couple of times you just used the pool or sauna, the occasion when you'd forgotten your trainers and the times you couldn't run because you'd pulled a calf muscle and, let's face it, you've barely burned off the calories of a roast potato.

Failure in most cases results from a combination of over-adventurous expectation and the complete absence of a plan.

Rather than reinventing ourselves, we should be thinking in terms of a plan to make the best of who we are. Although the changes we make will be incremental rather than seismic, having a realistic view of what can be achieved might eventually end with some satisfaction rather than disappointment.

Getting started

Three steps to successful planning:

- Get conscious.
- Plan to plan.
- Tick the box of achievement.

You need to be in the frame of mind to change the way things are currently, then you have to make the effort to set some time aside and when it's in your diary you can cross that off your 'things to do' list.

The key to planning successfully is to view it like removing a sticking plaster: peeling slowly doesn't reduce the pain, it just draws it out over a longer period. Take the short, sharp, shock approach and it may hurt like mad at first but it's soon over.

Planning starts here

Take an hour to complete this stage. What you are aiming to do would take most organizations several days, but you simply don't have that amount of time to waste.

Because of this you will need to focus on the task in hand without any distractions. Choose somewhere quiet, switch phones to voicemail, turn off the computer, make sure you're fed and watered.

It is now vitally important for you to check your watch – you must take no more and no less than an hour for this task.

There are five stages to complete, including time for a short review at the end of the hour. Dividing the time up in advance is a good discipline and helps you to keep focused on the particular task you are working on.

The planning stages are as follows:

1. Audit
2. Make time

3. Target – macro planning and micro planning
4. Resourcing
5. Assessment.

And they fit into your planning hour like this:

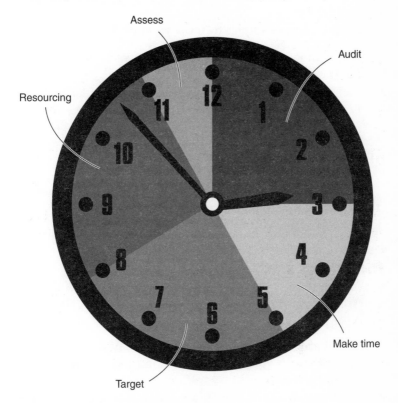

The stages of planning

Audit

This is the phase that answers the question 'where am I now?'
There will be a gap between where you are and where you
want to be, so this exercise is about identifying the ways that
can be bridged.

You need to work out your **feelings** and your **actions**.

We'll take it as read that you're not a hopeless case and that
there are some aspects of your communication that you are

happy about. However, as we're trying to address the negatives it inevitably means you have to face up to some of the things that currently bother you.

Try to come up with three statements that sum up how you feel about some of the weaker parts of your personal communication profile.

Here are a few examples to show what we mean:

■ 'I sometimes come out of meetings feeling as though I didn't really have my say.'
■ 'I seem to spend half of my day reading e-mail attachments.'
■ 'I can't seem to conquer my public speaking nerves.'

It's most likely that the issues that are most important to you will surface and that in itself is a good measure of what you'd like to address.

Being aware of your feelings is part of the process, but to stop it getting too unfocused you also need to look at the practical issues of how you spend your communications time.

Planning audit checklist
■ How many meetings do you attend each day/week?
■ What is the average duration of meetings?
■ What percentage of meetings takes more than an hour?
■ What percentage of meetings overrun?

■ How many e-mails do you receive per day/week?
■ How often do you deal with e-mail (once a day, hourly, when it arrives?)
■ What percentage of e-mails are action orientated vs. information giving?
■ What percentage of incoming e-mails is badly targeted/not relevant to you?
■ How often do you send e-mail (once a day, hourly, respond immediately?)

■ How many presentations (to more than six people) do you do?
■ What level of preparation do you make?
■ How many other people are available to help you prepare?

- How much time do you spend on the phone each day?
- What's the average call duration?
- How many calls are vital?
- Do you set aside a time of day for outgoing calls or do them as needed?

Conclusion

Most definitely the conclusion you will have come to is that you are wasting too much time on things that aren't important. If we knew this was going to be the case then why make you go through the exercise in the first place?

The answer is that once again you need to raise your own level of consciousness so that you can become better at what you do, and the exercise has the added benefit of starting to focus your mind on just which meetings are pointless, which e-mails irrelevant and phone calls unnecessary.

The trouble with meetings

Every meeting you have has a start time, but rarely, if ever, do they have an end time (unless everyone is booked to go to another meeting later that day!).

We know that work expands to fill the time there is to do it, but if we were to reverse things and treat the time as the important thing and not the work the miraculous result is that we would find huge chunks of it were freed up to do other stuff.

A meeting with no end time results in it meandering this way and that, drifting off at pointless tangents and not always finding its way back to the original purpose. Our minds mirror this journey, resulting in concentration lapsing and decision making becoming difficult if not impossible.

If at the start of the meeting you were to say, 'Okay we have half an hour to decide the best way of winning a new order from our biggest customer', you would be sure to stay focused and come up with more creative answers.

Time to think

Imagine that time is a bag full of sweets. Every day you are given a fresh bag and each delicious sweet represents 10 minutes of your valuable time.

All the tasks you are asked to perform can by represented by people who want some of your time/sweets (to reply to their e-mail, to attend their meeting or answer their phone call).

Each time you consent to their request you have to reach into the bag and give them the number of sweets that makes up their time allocation.

You can never take any of the sweets back, so if you give them all away (or pledge them to other people) then every day you will run out and still have left someone disappointed.

However, if you find ways of hanging onto your sweets so that by half way through the day everyone is satisfied and you have no more requests coming in then you have earned yourself free time.

You could choose to use it to help someone else out, or to start some of tomorrow's tasks or, luxury of all luxuries, to stop and think.

Tough decisions

You need to complete three steps to make more time.

First of all, you have to start to ask questions about all of those daily requests for sweets and come up with some reasons for allocating them. You have to decide on the difference between essential communication and nice-to-have.

Ask yourself some of these things:

■ What do I get out of this meeting? What do others get from my being there?
■ How much of the e-mail that I receive is relevant? How much is personal or non-work related? Would it be a good thing to ban this completely?
■ Who rings me just to catch up with gossip? What proportion of my overall time on the phone is focused on things that make a difference?
■ Are there people who ask my opinion more because they are lazy than because they really value it?
■ What kind of communication should I have with the people who work for me? What is the split between information and motivation? What are their expectations?

■ How often does my boss need an update? What level of detail is needed? What is the best communication channel (face to face, e-mail, phone call, Post-It note)?

Answer these questions and you will have taken the first important step to allocating your time, which is assessing the criteria for communication.

Who's in control?

Your boss has a dull monotone voice, wanders off the subject all the time and has no idea how to control the flow of an agenda, so why would you want to go to his weekly meeting? It could be because he's the boss.

This illustrates the issue of control. You may have decided who you want to communicate with and the most efficient channels but you have to take account of the other party too.

You can use this matrix to plot your planning.

Low control	High control	
Grin and bear it, you really need this stuff	Make the most of it	**Important and relevant**
Make an attempt to manage as well as you can	Get rid Jettison Eject Quit	**Trivial and irrelevant**

170 ■ Planning for success

Take some action

In the areas of high control you should be thinking about how you can make the most of the opportunities you have. Are you really using your time well, is there a way of shortening meetings, could you add other elements to make them more interesting to more participants?

Equally when it comes to decisions about what you get rid of, you can afford to be brutal; it's within your control.

Much more difficult to manage are the areas of low control – your boss probably won't take too kindly to being told his meetings stink, but that doesn't mean you should give up altogether. Maybe your peers feel the same and over time you might, with gentle persuasion and coercion, be able to bring about some changes.

Target

You now know how you feel about elements of the communication mix that you want to improve upon. Also, you have freed up some time and had another reminder of the practical things that work for you and the ones that don't.

From this you need to target three areas for improvement, taking into account both **action** and **frequency**.

This initial plan will drive how much ongoing planning you need to do because if you choose three simple actions that only need to be implemented once then you will have fulfilled the plan, then guess what? You need to start again. (Re-read Russell Grossman's quote at the beginning of the chapter if you need convincing.)

Some things might take longer to implement and there may be an ongoing commitment, which eats into some of your time on a weekly or even daily basis.

Here are some examples of actions you might think about – see how the frequency affects the overall level of commitment you have to make:

■ I am going to improve my presentation skills by enrolling on a public speaking course at college.

■ I am going to spend the last 30 minutes of the working day tidying the e-mail inbox, managing incoming mail into files and deleting any redundant messages.

■ I am going to source one new trade magazine, industry publication, newspaper or periodical per week with information relevant to my job. Then I'm going to take one hour per week to read and digest the publication, taking notes on content and learning as appropriate.

■ I am going to e-mail all my friends who send me junk mail or funny stuff and ask them to redirect future messages to my home account.

■ I am going to use my voicemail only in emergencies.

■ I am going to restrict all my team meetings to a maximum of one hour and produce an agenda in advance.

If there are dozens of things you want to achieve and you're afraid you're only tackling a few then remember that this isn't a one-off process. You're just choosing the highest priorities and the more progress you make with them, the sooner you'll be able to move onto your 'b' and 'c' list issues.

For the time being, you can afford to be adventurous in your thinking and take some risks in this safe environment; after all, until you reach the implementation stage it's only you who is being affected by the decisions. Look at the next section and you'll get some idea of what will be needed to help you achieve your objectives; if it looks too daunting then come up with more manageable targets.

Resourcing

The final part of the planning process is to look at how you are actually going to carry out the plan.

What are the resources you'll need to deliver your objectives? This might be a combination of physical evidence, as in the earlier case of the trade magazines, or you may need the help of colleagues, if you like, your human resources.

Here's a final checklist in this chapter to help spark your ideas:

■ Will I need to retrain? Who can help with that?

■ How and where can I source the physical evidence I need? (Consider logistics, cost, sharing the resources with others.)

■ What research tools are available (Internet, internal documentation etc.)?

- When will I know that I'm making progress, what checks can I put in place?
- Is there anyone who I can turn to as a mentor?
- Who are my role models?

Assessment

With five minutes left of your planning hour you should be taking time to look back at the process. This is simply to check that you managed to do what you promised:

- Have you successfully audited your current position?
- Do you know what kind of communicator you are and where your weaknesses lie?
- Are the time-wasting activities now apparent?
- Have you thought which ones you can jettison?
- Have you been able to come up with some objectives that are achievable?
- Are there some actions set against each of them?
- Have you identified who and what can help, as well as considering things like cost, timescale and logistics?

If you've achieved only 75 per cent of this, you will still have a workable plan – there will be things you can be getting on with right away. Rather than worrying about the remaining 25 per cent, use the last minute of your hour to diary some more planning time within the next month. Think about where the gaps are and jot a few notes down about what and how you'd like to fill them in your next planning session (it might mean gathering some resources in the intervening period).

Now that you've finished, you can tick your planning phase off the list and start on implementation.

Golden rules of planning

- Plan to plan – if you don't it won't happen.
- Do it quickly – keep it focused, that way you'll remember it better and it won't be nearly so painful.
- Planning is dull – achievement is enjoyable. So see planning as part of the process of achieving a shift in your skills.

- You can only feel good about your plan if you believe in it.
- At any one time you can only wear one pair of shoes – concentrate on the task in hand and get round to the others later.
- Apply an elevator test to your plan – could you describe it to a colleague in a few short sentences?
- Construct a planning cycle that includes time for review and reflection – then you can make the next stage of your plan.
- Write it down – pin it up. Keep the fact that you have a plan to achieve at the front of your mind, even if you have to attach it to the inside of the fridge door.

A planning example
Shooting a video

How much planning would you put into the shooting of a short video for your next company conference? Say the CEO wants to present a piece to camera, followed by footage of the manufacturing plant and then some customers buying the end product.

You're working alongside the producer who will cover all the technical and creative aspects, but between you, you need to plan the logistics. Here are a few things you might have to consider: the length of the final piece and overall cost, which budget lines are essential and which just 'nice to have', availability of the CEO, a location which is quiet and fit for purpose, access to the manufacturing plant, health and safety issues, production insurance, permission to film customers, how and where to edit your footage, what format to produce it on (VHS, DVD etc).

All of this is just scratching the surface. Stop now and count off on the fingers of one hand just five extra things you can think of that would form part of the planning stage.

With a 'glamorous' piece of communication like video it is tempting to jump ahead, straight to the point when the camera starts to roll, but you can already start to see how much pre-work has to go on in order to deliver the finished product. If you logged all the hours needed to complete the project you would find that between a half and two-thirds would be taken in the planning and preparation stages.

The bigger the communication the greater the need is to plan. In the case of the video, taking short cuts will at best result in an inferior product, or at worst the collapse of the project altogether.

Try this

Planning is an example of an activity that is best tackled quickly using maximum concentration. None of us can sustain this kind of intense working across a whole day.

Under these circumstances you have to prepare yourself to make sure you achieve what you set out. The first thing is to put a time limit on the period of concentration (good teachers don't sustain the same activity for more than 20 minutes without some kind of break, we wouldn't recommend more than an hour on any one task).

Next, make sure there can be no distractions, firstly from the things we've mentioned like phones ringing and people calling by your office, but also you need to be clear-headed. It's no good sitting down to intense activity if there is an important and urgent task hanging over you.

Finally, and this may seem unrelated, drink lots and lots of water. There's increasing scientific evidence to suggest that many of us are often dehydrated and there is a direct correlation between this state and our powers of concentration.

The truth about... big plans and daily plans

Now you've looked at your overall communication strategy and drawn up a plan to keep it on track. The difficulty will be sustaining this on a daily basis when faced with all the other tasks that have to be done.

Lots of people fail because they don't have a daily plan. Making a things-to-do list is a good start, but if you have no sense of priority it's of little use. To be really effective you need to build in two additional factors. Firstly, you need to put a time allocation next to each item, otherwise how will you ever know if there are enough hours in the day to do what you have to? This time allocation should be in the form of 10-minute time slots (there's not much you can do in less than 10 minutes) and you shouldn't have any task that is more than an hour.

If you have a huge project that will take many hours to complete you need to allocate one-hour time slots to it, calling each a different thing as in this way you will feel a greater sense of achievement that you have moved further towards completing it.

Next, you have to put a number next to each item so that you have a chronological order to follow. In doing this you should balance the tasks against each other, so if you have a period of intense concentration, you should then do something that is less taxing. Don't be afraid to include routine tasks on the list, as they still take up your valuable time.

Here's an example of a structured things-to-do list:

1. Re-list tasks (1)
5. Check hotel availability for Thursday (1)
3. Prep production meeting report (2)
4. Write production meeting report (3)
7. E-mail Emma re: costings (1)
6. Reply to Ben with suggestions of agenda items (3)
10. Research competitor activity online (6)
9. Send thank you note to the team (2)
8. Write up meeting report for M.D. (6)
2. Sort and action incoming post (2)
11. Sort and action e-mail inbox (2)

The number down the right-hand side is the length of time (in 10-minute units) that you have allocated to each task, so there's an hour for the research activity, but only 20 minutes to sort out the post. This isn't an exact science – yes, you can decide that you're only going to spend half an hour writing up the production meeting report, but you have no idea what's in your e-mail inbox. Over time you will get better at predicting how much each item will need, but if you set yourself just 20 minutes to clear the e-mail it's surprising how much it focuses your mind.

Most people's levels of concentration are higher in the morning so you should plan to do the difficult tasks then.

In between the heavy stuff, like the report writing, you have allowed yourself either a reward (saying thank you to the team is a good thing to do and will make you feel better as a people manager), or what we'd call mindless tasks, like checking the hotel availability for example – they take very little concentration but allow you a break of sorts.

Incidentally, you are allowed proper breaks for a coffee or lunch as well!

To recap, there are three stages to making your list. First, write down the tasks to be done, next, allocate a time frame (in 10-minute segments), then finally, number the list in the order you will take things.

One final word on the way you allocate your time: it's good to make a habit of repetitive tasking. We can learn a lot from the production line techniques introduced by the Ford Motor Company. If you do all of the same type of thing one after another you get into a rhythm, which increases efficiency. It's much better than hopping from one thing to another. Just remember to build in a balance so that you don't go mad with the monotony.

According to...

Professor Cary Cooper

> You should start every day with a things-to-do list.
> I ask myself what's really important today and I put it in priority order, then I look at everything that comes in throughout the day, both electronic and hard copy, and I decide if any of these things should change my list – and if the answer is no then you leave it to the side and get on with your list. If something comes in that is really vital and supersedes your list items then you put it in.

Try this

Get hold of an extra A4-size diary for your things-to-do lists.

This has a number of benefits. Firstly it's great for medium- and longer-term planning as you can flick ahead through the diary and put tasks in for a day, a week or even several months hence. That's particularly useful for setting aside conscious planning time at regular intervals.

Also, you'll be better able to track your progress through tasks by looking back to see how many you get through in an average day – in time, your daily plans will get more efficient as you become more accurate in allocating time slots to different functions.

Finally, it'll shame you into doing the things you hate but are part of your job. This is because you transfer any incomplete tasks forward each day and the constant reminder of the things you put off should prompt you into action.

If you're really smart you'll put in all the family birthdays too!

The elevator test for Chapter 11

Planning is the first step to achieving our goals.

Short intense bursts of planning make it less of a chore.

Time is both finite and valuable – be careful how you allocate it.

Make your objectives manageable and give yourself a chance of hitting your targets.

Get into the daily habit of making a prioritized, time-allocated, things-to-do list.

Try to allocate the most difficult tasks to the morning, leaving the afternoon for less taxing routine tasks.

12

Six simple strategies

Where do you go from here? Now you know what the panel of experts thinks, you've digested the theory of better communication, you've even set out a plan for the future, all that's left is a reminder of what you'll need to help carry it out. This final chapter summarizes the learning of the six most important points in the text.

Think about your audience

Whether it's a room full of expectant faces waiting for you to impart some vital information or a chat with a junior colleague at the coffee machine, you need to pay equal attention and respect to where they are coming from.

Try to actively listen and get a real understanding of the motivations, aspirations and fears of the other party. Consider their ideals, their lifestyle, job function, background and prejudices; be sensitive to their view of you. Do they loathe you as the boss who is only there to make their lives hell? Or maybe they hang on your every word, respecting your views and experience. The worst mistake ever is when you think it's the latter and it's really the former!

Convey conviction

None of us is right all of the time, but you will earn great respect from people if you can truly convince them that you have belief in your ideas.

If you think something is right then say so, with passion. With experience you can learn to harness the power of that passion. Try to make sure that you keep your arguments well founded in logic and back them with the zeal that you really feel.

This conviction is a very powerful persuader and you can carry people along with you on a wave of enthusiasm. Be sure that you keep an eye on your goals and make everyone aware when you've achieved them, so that they get to experience for themselves the benefits of conviction.

One thing's certain, if you don't feel passionate about what you're doing, you're in trouble; no one is going to follow you if they think you are half-hearted about the job in hand. It is impossible to sustain any kind of enthusiasm for an idea you don't agree with.

'Shut up and listen'

Resist the urge to rush in with your own opinion until you've heard the facts. Which of us hasn't at some time lost our temper, only to find that the subject of our anger is a failing on our part? There is nothing more humbling than blaming someone else for failure, only to find that it's our fault. So it is with communication.

It's much easier to formulate ideas that are acceptable, if we've listened to the other party first. Try too to resist the temptation simply to *appear* attentive, instead make the effort to really hear what the other person is saying and meaning.

Stay conscious – think and plan

Don't drift along taking things as they come. Your planning should have helped you do this, but it's really easy to see that as a 'once-only' exercise and it is precisely that attitude which stops us from continually assessing where we're up to.

It'll help if you book more planning time in a physical sense by blocking the time out in your diary, but also on a daily basis try to take five minutes before you go home to think about what you've achieved with your communication.

Were you clear from the start about your purpose? Did people get the message? How well did you manage incoming communication, how efficient were you?

At an even more detailed level, do a spot check every now and then on how you handled a phone call, whether your reply to an e-mail was efficient and economical without being cold, if you made the points you wanted to at a meeting.

The great thing about being conscious of all these things is that it gives us the freedom and the power to make choices. We decide the best use of our own time and in doing that we free ourselves up from the effects of other people's poor communication.

The flip side is when we take things as they come, because then others are making choices for us, they're filling our inbox, allocating us tasks, getting their own way, and the result is energy-sapping and unfulfilling. Remember, stay conscious, actively conscious.

Be sensitive to culture

This takes the job of understanding your audience a step further. You're not just responding to the group of individuals within your vicinity, but in the wider environment. It's important to see this both on a company and country level, so as you move from one organization to another, try to pick up on the differences quickly. If you're transported to another part of the world it's even more vital that you understand custom and practice.

Use your listening skills and ask lots of questions. You'll be forgiven for a genuine mistake, but not for cultural arrogance, if you make it appear that yours is the 'right' way, simply because of where you're from.

Recognize the importance of storytelling

From an early age stories play an important part in our lives, but the tales we hear in childhood aren't just there to amuse us, they pass on important messages that define the society we live in; they are our first experience of the triumph of good over evil, of what's right and wrong.

Maybe the most significant part of storytelling is the way it embeds a message in our memory, so that we can recount the learning many years later.

In business a good story can have the same effect, with some added benefits. It can remove the attention from us as the storyteller and place it on the characters; they then become the expert or the fall guy. Conversely, when we want it to we can use it to focus attention on ourselves and make us the 'victim' of the story, which is something many skilled communicators do to show they are vulnerable and to develop empathy with their audience.

Think about the stories you already know; make a conscious effort to collect more as you go along and practise telling them in a safe environment (to friends in a social situation or to a couple of colleagues over a coffee), before you use them as the pivotal point of a major presentation.

These are the strategies we think are important; they draw on the experience of all our contributors and will go a long way to making your communication persuasive, understandable and well respected, and most of all it will make other people want to communicate back and that is at the core of all successful business.

Our last piece of advice is this: be yourself. You had an opportunity earlier in the book to find out a bit more about who you are; use that knowledge and your natural person-ality, combine it with what you have read and enjoy more successful communication.

Appendix I

Further recommended reading

Argyle, M (1967) *The Psychology of Interpersonal Behaviour*, Penguin Books, London

Christie, B (1981) *Face to File Communication*, John Wiley & Sons, Chichester

Clutterbuck, D and Hirst, S (2002) *Talking Business: Making Communication Work*, Butterworth-Heinemann, Oxford

Covey, S (1999) *The 7 Habits of Highly Effective People*, Simon & Schuster, London

Dive, B (2002) *The Healthy Organization*, Kogan Page, London

Goleman, D (1998) *Working with Emotional Intelligence*, Bloomsbury, London

Grout, J and Perrin, S (2002) *Recruiting Excellence*, McGraw Hill, London

Haslam, C and Bryman, A (1994) *Social Scientists Meet the Media*, Routledge, London

Kline, N (1998) *Time to Think*, Cassell Illustrated, London

Seeley, M and Hargreaves, G (2003) *Managing in the Email Office*, Butterworth-Heinemann, Oxford

Smith, P B and Bond, M (1993) *Social Psychology Across Cultures*, Harvester Press, Brighton

Appendix II

A list of contributors

John Akers – Manager of the Birmingham Office of the National Family Mediation Service – also acts as a Relate Counsellor

Simon Armson – Chief Executive of Samaritans

Chris Brewster – Professor of International Human Resource Management at South Bank University in London

Michael Broadbent – Director of Group Corporate Affairs, HSBC Holdings plc

David Clutterbuck – Visiting Professor at Sheffield Hallam University

Cary Cooper – BUPA Professor of Organizational Psychology at UMIST

Bill Dalton – CEO of HSBC Bank plc

Keith Edelman – Managing Director of Arsenal FC and former Chief Executive of Storehouse plc

Val Gooding – CEO of BUPA

Russell Grossman – Head of Internal Communications at the BBC

Keith Harris – Chairman of Seymour Pierce Group Plc and former Chairman of the Football League

Derek Hatton – former Labour politician, now a broadcaster and motivational speaker

Surinder Hundal – Internal Communications Director of Nokia

Chris Major – Head of PR at AstraZeneca

Lynn Rutter – Change Manager, Global HR Projects, Oxfam

Peter Sanguinetti – former Director of Corporate Communications, British Gas

Jan Shawe – Director of Corporate Communications, Sainsbury's Supermarkets Limited

Doug Simkiss – Consultant Paediatrician at the Birmingham Community Children's Centre

Alistair Smith – Chairperson of Alite Ltd, a company which specializes in development work in and around the fields of motivation, teaching and learning

Simon Terrington – founding director of Human Capital, a consultancy that advises media companies on their creative strategies

Kay Winsper – Head of Great Company at Microsoft

Index

Ackers, John 104
advertising 72–73
  car company case study 77–79
  and communication 83–84
  and creativity 76–77
  effectiveness 75–76
  TV commercials 84–85
  writing copy 77–82
'advertising puff' 82–83
Akers, John 8, 16, 118, 147, 149
Angus, Michael 150
appearance 143–44
Armson, Simon 103, 107, 148, 149, 150
attention span 135
audience 73–75, 178

bad news, breaking 24–25
Beckham, David 13
body language 106, 145–48
Brewster, Chris 11, 55, 142, 148, 155
Broadbent, Michael 91
bullet points 101

carpenter's rule 67–68
charisma 11, 12, 13
children, qualities of 16–18
Cinzano Bianco 77
Clutterbuck, David 12, 23, 108, 133, 137
communication
  and advertising 83–84
  and relationships 117–18
communication mix 170
communication problems 22–23
communication skills, self-assessment 27–32
confidence 32–34
consciousness earlier 179–80
control 169–70
conviction 179
Cooper, Cary 34, 47, 53, 112, 138, 176
creativity 76
cultural differences 148, 150–53, 180
culture 148–49
  comparison case study 156–57
  and touching 148–50
cut-the-crap cards 61

Dalton, Bill 86, 89–90, 153
Dictaphones 36
dictator type 27
digital on-screen graphics (DOGS) 135
double agent type 26–27

e-mail 45, 86–93
  benefits 90–92
  problems 87–90
Edelman, Keith 74–75
elevator test 3, 25, 37, 52, 69–70, 85, 101–02, 110, 116, 140, 158, 177
Emotional Intelligence: why it can matter more than IQ 14
empathy 11, 14–15, 157–58
eye contact 106, 146

face-to-face meetings 43–45
failure 163–64
feedback 34–36
First Direct 118–19
first impressions, non-verbal communication 141–42
Ford, Henry 72

Goleman, David 14
Gooding, Val 17, 35–36
gossip columnist type 27
Grossman, Russell 20, 73, 111, 161

Harper, David 57
Harris, Keith 11, 74, 90
Hatton, Derek 9, 13, 22, 23, 113, 143
honesty 9, 10
humour 15
Hundal, Surinder 91–92, 95, 97–98, 151

individual style 26–27
information overload 72
Internet 52–53
  writing for 98–101

kitchen sink type 27

letters 45
listening 15, 103–10, 179
  general rules 104–05
  how to listen 103–07

natural interest   105–07
when to listen   108–09

Major, Chris   93, 129, 130
meetings   43–5, 129–34, 167
post-meeting afterglow   134
preparation   129–31, 132–33
when to contribute   131–32
'mentors'   35, 67
'merit analysis'   44–45
mirroring   106, 147
mouse type   27

non-verbal communication   141–58
first impressions   141–42

organizational culture   153–56

passion   15–16
personal communication plan   161–63
persuasion   71–73
Plain English   57–59, 60, 61
planning   161–77, 164–65, 179–80
assessment   172
audit stage   165–67
example (shooting a video)   173–74
resourcing   171–72
rules of   172–73
target   170–71
things-to-do list   174–77
PowerPoint   137–39
presentations   134–39
expectations   136

questions   34–36

Ratner, Gerald   10–11
reading   47–53
assessing information   49–51
selection of material   47–49
when to read   51
relationships
and communication   117–18
starting   42–45
Rutter, Lynn   10, 21, 48–49, 151, 152

Samaritans   107
Sanguinetti, Peter   56
secret agent type   26
self improvement   163–64
self-assessment, communication skills   27–32
self-awareness   14
self-doubt   33
Shawe, Jan   68, 162
Simkiss, Doug   7–8, 24–5

sincerity   181
Smith, Alistair   17, 19, 71–72, 136–37, 145
spark   16
'spin'   56–57
starting relationships   42–45
story writing   59–61
storytelling   19–22, 181

talking   111–16
delivery   112–14
rehearsed and unrehearsed speech   115
techniques   114
target audiences   73–75, 178
telephone
ad hoc approach   42–43
familiar calls   128–29
first calls   126–27
first impressions   42–43
inbound calls   120–21
outbound calls   126–29
planned approach   43
voicemail   121–22
techniques   123–26
telephone banking   118–20
Terrington, Simon   34, 109, 131, 139, 144, 147
texting   94–98
criteria for   95–98
Thatcher, Margaret   23
things-to-do list   174–77
time management   167–68
touch-typing   93
touching, and culture   148–50
trust   7
truth   7–11
TV commercials   84–85

Winsper, Kay   65–66, 156
wit   15
writing
advertising copy   77–82
bullet points   101
context   62
establishing personality   55–57
for the Internet   98–101
letters   69
Plain English   57–59, 60, 61
presentation   62–63
reading and checking   67–68
spelling and grammar   65–68
story writing   59–61
structure   63–64
tone of voice   64–65